EYEWITNESS BOOKS

PYRAMID

Gold jackal, probably from Nubia, 1st century B.C.

Pyramidion of Bugentef, New Kingdom

Olmec stone mask

Gold plaque with the name of a Nubian king

Model adze and saw from the reign of Thutmose III, 1479-1425 B.C.

Foreman Anherkhau and his son

Bronze
ram-headed
sphinxes
from Nubia

EYEWITNESS BOOKS

PYRAMID

Written by
JAMES PUTNAM

Photographed by
GEOFF BRIGHTLING & PETER HAYMAN

Hetepheres and
her husband
Katep, C 2500 B.C.

Two plaques
with name of
Nubian King
Aspelta

Stoddart

Carving from Tomb of Ti, Saqqara

Nubian pot decorated
with blue lotuses

Jewellery found near the pyramid
of Senusret III, 1874–1855 B.C

DK

A DORLING KINDERSLEY BOOK

Project editor Scott Steedman
Art editor Manisha Patel
Managing editor Simon Adams
Managing art editor Julia Harris
Production Catherine Semark
Researcher Céline Carez
Picture research Cynthia Hole
Editorial consultant Dr I.E.S. Edwards

This Eyewitness ™ Guide has been conceived by
Dorling Kindersley Limited and Editions Gallimard

First published in Canada in 1994 by
Stoddart Publishing Co. Limited,
34 Lesmill Road, Toronto, Canada M3B 2T6

First published in Great Britain in 1994
by Dorling Kindersley Limited,
9 Henrietta Street, London WC2E 8PS

Canadian Cataloguing in Publication Data

Putnam, James
Pyramid

(Eyewitness books)
ISBN 0-7737-2810-4

1. Pyramids – Juvenile literature. I. Brightling, Geoff.
II. Hayman, Peter. III. Title. IV. Series.

DT63.P87 1994   j932'.01   C94–931129–4

Color reproduction by Colourscan, Singapore
Printed in Singapore by Toppan

Shabti figure of King Aspelta
of Nubia, 593–568 B.C.

Model of King
Khufu's funerary boat

Contents

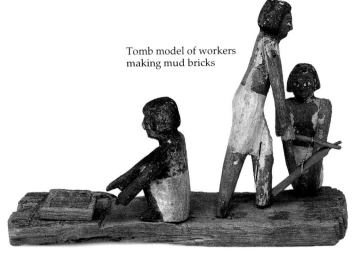

Tomb model of workers
making mud bricks

6
What are pyramids?
8
Built for a king
10
The great Step Pyramid
12
The Step Pyramid complex
14
First true pyramids
16
The pyramids of Giza
18
The pharaohs of Giza
20
The Great Pyramid
22
Inside the pyramid
24
Temples and offerings
26
The Sphinx
28
Funeral boats
30
Planning the pyramid
32
Building in brick and stone
34
Tools for building

36
The pyramid rises
38
A slow decline
40
The Middle Kingdom revival
44
Pyramidions
46
Riddles of the pyramids
48
Pyramids of Nubia
50
Pharaohs of Nubia
52
A queen's treasure
54
Pyramids of Mexico
56
Mayan pyramids
60
Aztec pyramids
62
The pyramid lives on
64
Index

What are pyramids?

THE PYRAMIDS OF EGYPT have fascinated people for thousands of years. How did the ancient Egyptians build these massive stone monuments, and why? The most famous pyramids are the three at Giza, near modern Cairo. But there are more than 80 other pyramids in Egypt, and another 100 farther south in the Sudan. Experts believe each one is a tomb, built by a pharaoh (king) as the final resting place for his body. The pyramid was meant to help the dead pharaoh achieve eternal life. But we may never know why the Egyptians chose the pyramid shape. It may have developed from early burial mounds, or been a symbol of the sun's rays or of a stairway to heaven. Many centuries later, the people of Central America built pyramids, mainly as temples. Hundreds of these are still hidden in the deep jungles.

THE GREAT SPHINX
The period we call ancient Egypt lasted for 3,000 years. The Giza pyramids and the Sphinx (pp. 26–27) were built early on, during the Old Kingdom (c. 2613–2160 B.C.). Pyramid building was revived in the Middle Kingdom (2040–1750 B.C.). By the New Kingdom (1550–1086 B.C.), pharaohs (including Tutankhamun) were buried in secret underground rock tombs.

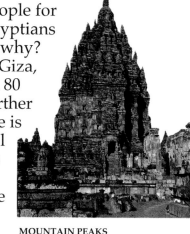

MOUNTAIN PEAKS
Buildings of worship all over the world have a pointed pyramid shape. Most cultures believe the gods live in the heavens, so earthly spirits can rise from temples to join them. Most temples, churches, synagogues, mosques, and pagodas have spires that rise like mountain peaks. This is the Temple of Siva in Prambanan in Java, Indonesia.

BLOODTHIRSTY SACRIFICE
The Aztecs of ancient Mexico built pyramid temples to worship their gods (pp. 60–61). Each temple had two staircases that led to two shrines. Aztec priests performed human sacrifices in the shrines to honor the forces of nature. They believed they could keep the sun alive only if they fed the gods human blood.

Aztec, Mayan, and other Central American pyramids

Egyptian and Sudanese pyramids

WORLDS APART
Pyramids are found in Egypt and Central America. But there is no evidence that the early Americans had any contact with Egypt, or even knew that the Egyptian pyramids existed. In both time and space, the two civilizations were worlds apart.

SPOT THE DIFFERENCE
This is the Mayan pyramid of Chichén Itzá in Mexico. Central American pyramids have flat tops and staircases on at least one side. Mayan priests climbed the stairs to reach the altar on the summit. Unlike the best Egyptian pyramids, which are made of solid limestone blocks, Central American pyramids are filled with layers of rubble.

STONE SUNBEAM
The pharaoh Khafra built this pyramid at Giza around 2520 B.C. It is only slightly smaller than the Great Pyramid, the biggest of them all (pp. 22–23). The pyramid shape resembles the rays of the sun shining through a break in the clouds. The tip may have been cased in gold to make it shine like the sun.

HIDDEN MOUND

The earliest Egyptian tombs were burial mounds. A simple grave was covered with a heap of gravel to protect it and mark the spot in the shifting desert sands. Later, kings and high officials were buried in mastabas, oblong buildings made of sun-dried mud bricks. Some mastabas had sand mounds overlaid with bricks over the burial chamber. This is the Step Pyramid of King Djoser, built around 2680 B.C. (pp. 12–15). It was the first pyramid, and the first king's tomb made of stone.

CHANGING SHAPE

The first Egyptian pyramids had stepped sides. These probably represented a stairway that the dead king could climb to join the other gods among the stars (pp. 22, 47). Later the sun became more important than the stars in Egyptian religion. Then they built true pyramids with sloping sides representing the sun's rays. This is the ruined Meidum pyramid (pp. 14–15). It was first built as a step pyramid, and was later modified to become a true pyramid.

Some of the high quality limestone facing is left near the summit

LIFE SOURCE

Every year the Nile River flooded and brought the Egyptians fresh, fertile soil. They believed that the world had been created as a mound rising from the primeval waters. The mound shape was thought to be the source of all life. Perhaps by copying its shape, the pyramid had magic powers to help the king be reborn.

Hundreds of thousands of limestone blocks laid in rows

SON OF THE SUN GOD

This painting shows a pharaoh and the sun god Re. In one spell from the pyramid texts (p. 22), the pharaoh tells Re: "I have laid down for myself those rays of yours as a stairway under my feet on which I will ascend." Re is shown as a man with a hawk's head. On top of his head is the sun, encircled by the serpent of time. He holds a scepter and the ankh, the emblem of life.

Built for a king

THE EGYPTIANS BELIEVED THEIR PHARAOH was a living god. He led the army in battle, passed judgment on criminals, and controlled the treasury. He also represented the unity of Egypt. In early times, most people lived in the north or the south, called Lower and Upper Egypt. It was the pharaoh's role to keep the two regions together. The centralized government meant he had all the resources of Egypt at his disposal for building his pyramid. The finest sculptors, masons, engineers, and countless workers spent years building the tomb. The laborers who dragged the stones were not slaves. They were farmers who believed that if they helped their king get to heaven, he would look after them in the next world.

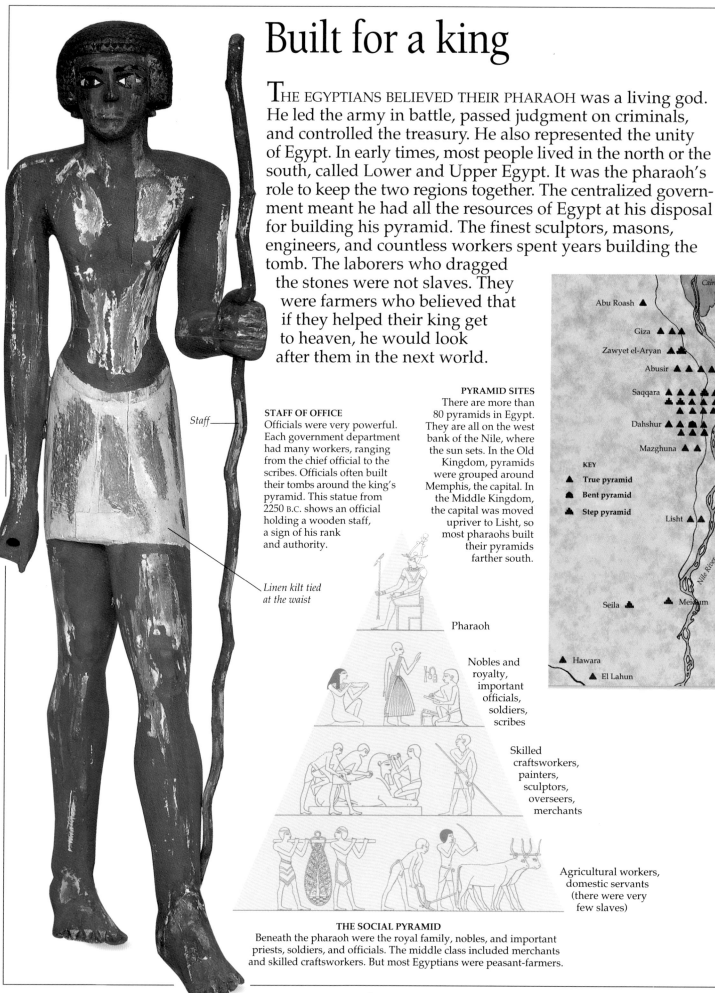

Staff

STAFF OF OFFICE
Officials were very powerful. Each government department had many workers, ranging from the chief official to the scribes. Officials often built their tombs around the king's pyramid. This statue from 2250 B.C. shows an official holding a wooden staff, a sign of his rank and authority.

Linen kilt tied at the waist

PYRAMID SITES
There are more than 80 pyramids in Egypt. They are all on the west bank of the Nile, where the sun sets. In the Old Kingdom, pyramids were grouped around Memphis, the capital. In the Middle Kingdom, the capital was moved upriver to Lisht, so most pharaohs built their pyramids farther south.

Cairo
Abu Roash ▲
Giza ▲ ▲ ▲
Zawyet el-Aryan ▲ ▲🔺
Abusir ▲ ▲ ▲
Saqqara ▲ ▲ ▲ ▲ 🔺🔺🔺 ▲▲▲
Dahshur ▲ ▲ ▲ 🔺▲ ▲▲
Mazghuna ▲ ▲

KEY
▲ True pyramid
🔺 Bent pyramid
🔺 Step pyramid

Lisht ▲ ▲

Seila 🔺   Meidum ▲

Hawara ▲
El Lahun ▲

Nile River

Pharaoh

Nobles and royalty, important officials, soldiers, scribes

Skilled craftsworkers, painters, sculptors, overseers, merchants

Agricultural workers, domestic servants (there were very few slaves)

THE SOCIAL PYRAMID
Beneath the pharaoh were the royal family, nobles, and important priests, soldiers, and officials. The middle class included merchants and skilled craftsworkers. But most Egyptians were peasant-farmers.

8

SON OF THE SUN GOD
The pharaoh had many official titles, including Lord of the Two Lands and Son of Re, the sun god. This huge head of Radjedef was found near his pyramid at Abu Roash. The king is wearing the royal *nemes* headcloth. A cobra is poised on his brow, ready to spit fire at the king's enemies. Radjedef ruled only for eight years, between Khufu and Khafra, who built the two massive pyramids at Giza. His pyramid is ruined.

Ancient Egyptian women carried trays and baskets on their heads

HUMBLE SERVANT
Many young women worked as servants. We know what they looked like because model figures of servants were put into tombs so that they could work for their bosses in the next life.

MODEL COUPLE
In Egyptian statues, pharaohs usually have elegant, perfect features. Ordinary people are more natural and realistic. This is the court official Katep and his wife Hetepheres. He has a suntan, but his wife has pale skin, suggesting that she spent most of her time indoors. The statue was found in Katep's tomb near the Giza pyramids.

Hetepheres with her arm around her husband

Katep, who lived around 2500 B.C.

Wig

Her skin is painted a pale yellow

His skin is painted red

The great Step Pyramid

IN THE SHADOW OF THE STEP PYRAMID
Over the following centuries, many important officials built their mastaba tombs around the mighty Step Pyramid. The walls are mostly decorated with everyday scenes. This carving comes from the tomb of the official Mereruka, c. 2300 B.C. It shows men carrying offerings of food, including ducks.

THE FIRST PYRAMID – probably the first large stone structure in human history – was built for the pharaoh Djoser at Saqqara around 2680 B.C. It was designed by the architect Imhotep, who became more famous than Djoser. The Step Pyramid is really a series of six mastabas, flat-roofed buildings with sloping sides set one on top of the other. Beneath it, cut deep into the underground rock, lie the burial chambers of Djoser and five members of his family. The king's vault was lined with granite and sealed with a three-ton plug. But it was robbed long ago – only a mummified foot was found inside.

A BUILDER'S SKETCH
This is an ancient architectural drawing, probably made by builders working on the Step Pyramid. The vertical lines allowed them to figure out the exact angle of the building's sloping sides.

BUILT IN STAGES
The Step Pyramid was built around a core of desert stones. Imhotep changed his mind five times as the building progressed. He enlarged the original mastaba form twice before building a four-tiered pyramid structure on top. Then two more tiers were added by expanding the entire structure. It was finally faced with polished limestone to give a smooth finish.

The body of the pyramid is made of small stone blocks laid like bricks

Imhotep

More than 2,000 years after his death, the ancient Egyptians worshiped Imhotep as a god of wisdom. One writer called him "the inventor of the art of building with hewn stone." He is said to have written many books and became a sort of patron saint of scribes. He is often shown seated with a papyrus unrolled across his knees. He was also thought to be the son of the god Ptah, whose magic gave him the power to heal the sick.

Bronze statue of
Imhotep, New Kingdom

UNFINISHED STATUE
This is one of three unfinished life-sized statues of Djoser found in his pyramid complex. Even in this worn state, the king's stern expression shows through. The spirit of a dead king was thought to emerge from the burial chamber and inhabit statues like these.

DISCOVERING THE WHEEL
How were the pyramids built? Did the Egyptians have building machines? There are many theories, but little hard evidence. This painting shows soldiers climbing a ladder on wheels. It is the only known image of a wheel from the Old Kingdom. At that time the Egyptians did not have pulleys for lifting stones.

Nemes headcloth

Thick wig

False beard

Fine Tura limestone facing was stolen for later buildings

THE KING'S PORTRAIT
The first life-sized portrait in history is this seated statue of King Djoser. It was found in a closed chamber attached to the north side of his pyramid. Two round holes in the wall allowed the pharaoh to see the offerings left by his worshipers. The king is wearing a *nemes* headcloth, a sign of royalty, oddly poised on top of a bushy wig. His eyes were once inlaid with rock crystal. The wear and tear of 4,700 years cannot hide the king's strong personality, seen in his fierce face, prominent cheekbones, thick lips, and heavy jaw.

One of Djoser's name in hieroglyphs

The Step Pyramid complex

HIS LIFE'S WORK
Born in 1902, Jean-Philippe Lauer is a French architect and Egyptologist. He spent 50 years reconstructing the Step Pyramid complex at Saqqara. When he began, in 1926, the ruined columns andshattered blocks of stone lay buried in the desert sand. The model on this page is the fruit of his life's work.

THE SAQQARA STEP PYRAMID was part of a large complex. Surrounding the pyramid is a series of courtyards and ceremonial buildings. Although they are small next to the pyramid, these were probably among the first large stone buildings ever made. Many are shaped and decorated like earlier structures of mud bricks, rushes, reeds, or wood. Though they are carved to look like real buildings, most of them are dummies, complete with fake doors. One courtyard was used for the special *sed* festival, held after Djoser had been king for many years. Crowds from all over Egypt came to watch the pharaoh run a course in the *sed* court. This makes the Step Pyramid the world's first sports arena! The race was a symbolic renewal of the king's power. Afterward, he was re-crowned as king of Upper and Lower Egypt on two thrones next to the *sed* court.

KIND OF BLUE
A small underground chamber lies to the south. The king was certainly buried under the pyramid, so the purpose of this second tomb is a mystery. The carvings and blue tiles may be a copy of the decoration in Djoser's palace at Memphis.

South tomb, a series of underground rooms entered by a steep descending shaft

The outer walls form a giant rectangle 1,800 ft (550 m) long and 900 ft (275 m) wide

Large south courtyard lined with columns and dummy buildings

False door, a huge structure that does not open

The only real door

Blue glazed tiles from the under-ground passages in the south tomb

STONE FLOWERS
These columns are along one wall of the House of the North. They were carved to look like papyrus plants, with triangular shafts like real stems. The capitals (tops) are shaped like open papyrus flowers. The Egyptians often copied nature in their architecture, so that it would blend into the living world.

Capitals shaped like papyrus flowers

STERN SUPPORT
A pavilion in the south courtyard was held up by these three columns. Statues may have stood in the alcoves between them.

The pyramid has six steps, reaching a final height of 198 ft (60 m)

Bottom step is 398 ft (121 m) long and 358 ft (109 m) across

House of the North

House of the South

A vast network of passages and the king's burial chamber lies under the pyramid

Dummy chapels, many with gently curved roofs

FALSE DOORS AND DUMMY HOUSES
The Step Pyramid complex is the first of its kind. It must have been designed by the architect Imhotep (pp. 10–11) under the watchful eye of King Djoser. The details and layout are very interesting, because many later pyramids copied them in various ways. Fifteen doors are cut into the imposing outer wall. But only one of these doors can be entered – the other 14 are fakes, with carved hinges that do not open. Most of the buildings inside are also dummies. Some have beautiful outside walls and roofs but are filled with rubble on the inside. The buildings were never meant to be used, and probably had a magical or religious significance. The complex may have been a full-scale model of the royal palace at Memphis, so that Djoser could continue to live like a king in the afterlife.

Rectangular pillars jut out of the walls every 13 ft (4 m)

The sed court, where King Djoser ran a course to prove that he was still fit to rule; he was watched by crowds from all of the political regions of Egypt

First true pyramids

THE PHARAOHS who followed King Djoser also built step pyramids. The familiar smooth pyramid shape was not developed until the reign of King Sneferu. In his 24 years as pharaoh (2575–2551 B.C.), he won wars in Libya and Nubia and built many new temples, fortresses, and palaces. Sneferu also built at least three – maybe even four – pyramids. His first, at Meidum, shows how building had progressed by that time. The construction of the core and outer casing is similar to Djoser's Step Pyramid. But the Meidum builders had made great advances in the handling of large blocks of stone. The main structure is made of huge slabs, not many small blocks. The builders had also devised a new way of roofing the burial chamber so it held the weight of the pyramid above and used improved methods of sealing the entrance against robbers. All these features were employed by Sneferu's son, Khufu, who built the biggest pyramid of all, the Great Pyramid of Giza. But in total tons of stone, Sneferu's four pyramids were an even bigger building project.

PYRAMID PROFESSOR
W. M. Flinders Petrie (1853–1942) was a brilliant English archeologist. Over 41 years, he excavated almost every major site in Egypt. He pioneered new scientific methods and published more than a thousand books and papers. Petrie made the first detailed study of the Giza pyramids, in 1881 and 82. He also figured out how the strange-looking Meidum Pyramid had been built.

THE DAHSHUR PYRAMIDS
Sneferu built two large pyramids at Dahshur. It is impossible to visit them now, because they are in a military zone. This old photo shows the Bent Pyramid, which the Egyptians called "the Gleaming Pyramid of the South." It has more of its fine stone facing than any other pyramid. The builders started at a very steep pitch. But halfway up they changed angles, probably because cracks appeared. The Bent Pyramid is also unusual in having two entrances, and two burial chambers – both empty. The northern pyramid was built later. It is a true pyramid that rises at a very flat angle.

PRINCE...
Some of Sneferu's family were buried by the Meidum pyramid. One tomb held these superb statues of Sneferu's son Prince Rahotep and his wife, Nofret.

...AND PRINCESS
The eyes are real glass. The statues are so realistic that when the workmen saw them for the first time, they dropped their tools and fled!

KILLER KING
Sneferu was the first king of the Fourth Dynasty. He was an ambitious pharaoh. This carving celebrates a raid on the turquoise mines at Maghara in the Sinai Peninsula. It shows Sneferu killing an enemy. The text calls him "a great god… who conquers the foreign lands."

FAMOUS GEESE

Sneferu's eldest son was called Nefer-Maat. He was buried with his wife, Atet, in a tomb next to the Meidum pyramid. The walls are painted with colorful scenes of daily life. This famous detail shows geese eating grass. Roasted geese were a great delicacy for the ancient Egyptians.

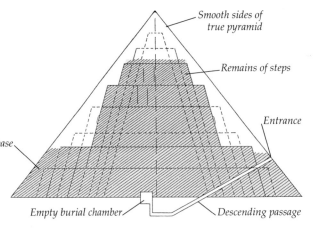

Smooth sides of true pyramid

Remains of steps

Entrance

Sand and remains of base

Empty burial chamber

Descending passage

AND ON THE INSIDE...

It is usually very hard to tell how a pyramid was made without taking it apart. But the Meidum Pyramid has collapsed enough to reveal its inner structure. It started off as a step pyramid with seven steps but was later enlarged to eight. Both versions have traces of fine limestone casing and were meant to be final. But in a final change of design, the steps were filled in to produce a true pyramid with smooth sides.

The Meidum Pyramid stands on the border between green farmland, the land of the living, and the desert, the land of the dead

DESERT TOWER

The Meidum Pyramid rises like a tower against the desert landscape. Only the inner core is left, surrounded by a pile of rubble. This picture shows the causeway leading to the entrance. This was the first pyramid Sneferu built, and it might have been started by an earlier king. Sneferu may have decided to convert it into a true pyramid when the Bent Pyramid started to crack. But the burial chamber was never finished. As it is farther south than any other Old Kingdom pyramid, it may have been a cenotaph – a memorial to the dead king.

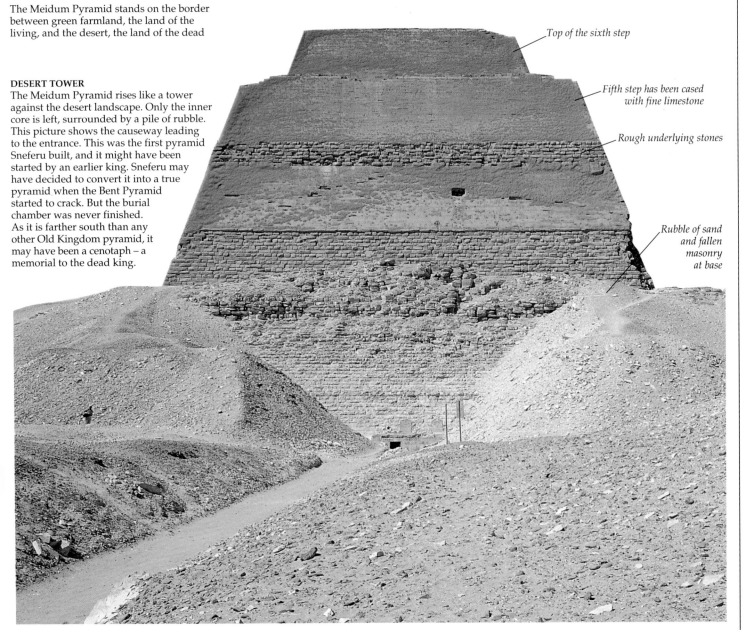

Top of the sixth step

Fifth step has been cased with fine limestone

Rough underlying stones

Rubble of sand and fallen masonry at base

The pyramids of Giza

"TIME LAUGHS AT ALL THINGS: BUT THE PYRAMIDS laugh at time." This old Arab proverb pays respect to the great pyramids of Giza, which have sat on a high plateau by the Nile for more than 4,500 years. By the time of Tutankhamun, they were more than a thousand years old, and even the Egyptians thought of them as ancient wonders. To the Arabs, who invaded Egypt in A.D. 639, the pyramids were unbelievably old. From a distance, they are an awesome, majestic sight. Up close, they are massive. The largest of the three, the Great Pyramid of King Khufu, was built around 2550 B.C. At its peak it was 481 ft (147 m) tall, with a square base 756 ft (230 m) on a side. It is made of about 2,300,000 blocks of solid limestone, each weighing 2.5 tons on average. Its neighbor, built 70 years later for King Khafra, is 9 ft (3 m) shorter. The third great pyramid was made for the pharaoh Menkaura. It is the smallest of the three, standing only 218 ft (66 m) high.

TOMBS BY THE NILE
Like all the major tombs of ancient Egypt, the Giza pyramids were built on the west bank of the Nile River. The Egyptians believed that this was the land of the dead. When the sun set in the west each day, they thought it traveled into another world where the spirits of dead kings lived.

THE RIDDLE OF THE SPHINX
The Great Sphinx (pp. 26–27) looks east toward the rising sun. Carved from a huge outcrop of limestone, it has the body of a crouching lion and the face of a king, probably Khafra. Some workers building Khafra's pyramid may have seen the shape in a piece of leftover rock. They probably carved it as a tribute to their king.

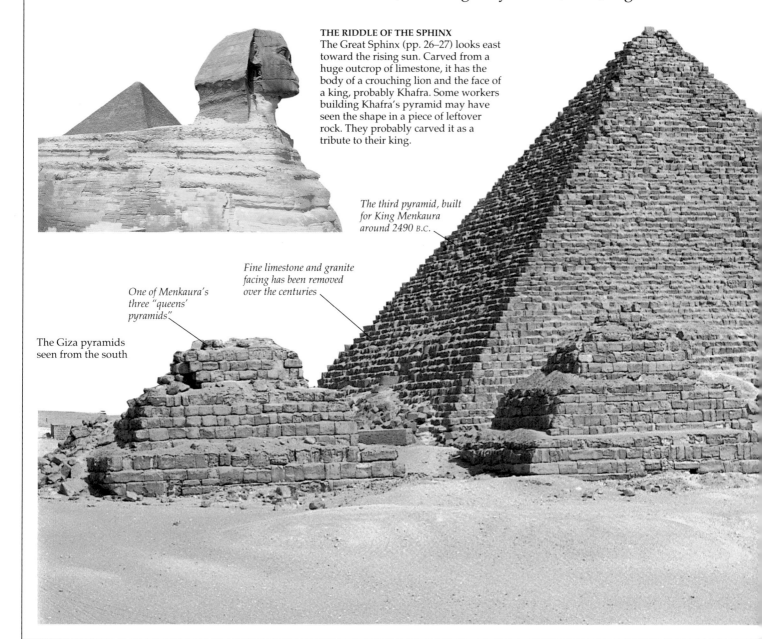

The third pyramid, built for King Menkaura around 2490 B.C.

Fine limestone and granite facing has been removed over the centuries

One of Menkaura's three "queens' pyramids"

The Giza pyramids seen from the south

BY CAMEL AROUND THE PYRAMIDS
For 4,500 years, people have come to see the great tombs of the pharaohs. Today millions of tourists from around the world visit the pyramids every year.

A GREAT VIEW
The best view of the Giza complex is from the top of the Great Pyramid. This picture comes from *Views in Egypt*, published by the Italian adventurer Luigi Mayer in 1804. It shows European travelers admiring the scenery from the summit. They are wearing Turkish dress, a common custom for travelers at the time.

The second pyramid, built for King Khafra around 2520 B.C.

Some of the fine Tura limestone facing is left near the summit

The top 33 ft (10 m) have been lost

Great Pyramid of Khufu

Khufu's queens' pyramids

Khafra's pyramid

Menkaura's pyramid

Queens' pyramids

Great Sphinx

THE WHOLE COMPLEX
This is an aerial view of the Giza pyramids. There are 10 pyramids in all, because all three pharaohs built at least one small pyramid beside their big pyramids. These smaller structures are usually called queen's pyramids, though only some of them were built for the pharaohs' wives (p. 19).

The Great Pyramid, biggest of them all, built for King Khufu around 2550 B.C.

The pharaohs of Giza

THE PHARAOH HAD TOTAL authority. His subjects thought of him as a god and would do anything for him. Without this absolute power, the pyramids could never have been built. The word *pharaoh* means "great house," and originally referred to the palace rather than the king. Khufu, Khafra, and Menkaura had their palaces at Memphis. From there they could admire their massive tombs being built nearby at Giza. The building process took many years – if the pharaoh was lucky, his pyramid would be ready before he died. These huge projects must have put an enormous strain on Egypt's economy. When they were finally finished, the Giza pyramids were given names which celebrated the majesty of the kings who built them. The Great Pyramid was called "Khufu is one belonging to the horizon." The other two were known as "Great is Khafra" and "Menkaura is divine."

RARE PORTRAIT
Khufu was probably the most powerful pharaoh ever to rule Egypt. Yet the only portrait of him to survive is this tiny ivory statue. When it was found, it had no head. The English archeologist Flinders Petrie had to sift through mounds of rubble before he finally found the missing head.

Pleated nemes headcloth

Royal beard

LION THRONE
One of the most striking Egyptian statues is this portrait of the pharaoh Khafra. He succeeded Khufu as king, and may have been Khufu's younger brother. The statue is carved from a shiny, mottled stone called diorite. The king is shown larger than life size sitting on a lion throne. The statue was found deep in a pit in Khafra's valley temple, part of his pyramid complex. It may have been hidden there to save it from destruction by thieves or enemies.

Pleated kilt

Lion head

FALCON POWER
A falcon perches on Khafra's throne, its outstretched wings wrapped around his throat. The bird represents Horus, the god associated with the supreme power and strength of the pharaoh.

HEAD IN THE SAND
The Great Sphinx (pp. 26–27) crouches in front of Khafra's pyramid. Its massive head is thought to be a portrait of the pharaoh. For most of its history, the Sphinx has been covered up to the neck in the drifting desert sands.

WE THREE KINGS
These are the cartouches – hieroglyphic names – of the three Giza pharaohs. Each name is framed by an oval loop of rope with a knot at the base. The loop represented eternity. By placing his name inside it, the pharaoh hoped to live forever.

Khafra's cartouche

| Khufu | Khafra | Menkaura |

The king has a muscular physique; his queen has much softer curves

MODEL COUPLE
Most Egyptian pharaohs had many wives. But only two or three were queens, and the king usually had a favorite. This is the earliest known statue of a king and queen together. They are Menkaura and his favorite wife, Khamerernebty. The queen is hugging her husband in an affectionate way. Human touches like this are rare in Egyptian art, which is very formal. There are no records about Menkaura from his own age. But Greek historians say he was a fair and just pharaoh. In contrast, they describe Khufu and Khafra as wicked tyrants who forced the whole country to work on their pyramids.

Menkaura's cartouche

The fine grain of the stone graywacke gives the sculpture a smooth finish

ANCIENT REPAIRS
A broken wooden coffin was found in Menkaura's pyramid. But the style and writing show that it was made nearly 2,000 years after the king's death. Later Egyptians must have tried to repair his coffin after it was damaged.

Queens' pyramids
King Menkaura built three smaller pyramids just south of his own pyramid. None of them was finished, but one is partly cased in granite. This is the largest of the three, where his queen Khamerernebty was probably buried. Many other pyramid complexes include smaller "queens' pyramids." But not all of them were built as tombs for the king's wives. Some were tombs for his daughters, and others seem to have had different, more symbolic purposes.

The Great Pyramid

THE LARGEST AND MOST FAMOUS PYRAMID is the Great Pyramid at Giza. It was built or King Khufu beginning around 2550 B.C. Tourists have come to marvel at it for the last 4,500 years. With its original casing of white limestone glittering in the sunlight, it must have been a truly awesome sight. Many people believe it is the greatest monument ever made. The base is bigger than any temple, cathedral, or mosque. Until the Eiffel Tower was finished in 1887, the Great Pyramid was also the tallest structure ever built. The precision of its construction is astonishing. The four sides, each slightly more than 755 ft (230 m) long, are aligned almost exactly with true north, south, east, and west. The difference between the longest and shortest sides is only 7.9 in (20 cm). This mountain of stone contains approximately 2,300,000 blocks, weighing a total of about 6,500,000 tons. Inside is a fascinating network of passages, shafts, galleries, and hidden chambers (pp. 22–23).

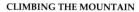

CLIMBING THE MOUNTAIN
The Arabs used to call the Great Pyramid "the Mountain of Pharaoh." In the 19th century, European tourists paid local guides to carry them to the top. This was very dangerous – people who slipped and fell were often killed. Writing in 1875, the American author Mark Twain said it was "a lively, exhilarating, lacerating, muscle-straining, bone-wrenching and perfectly excruciating and exhausting pastime." Nowadays climbing the pyramids is against the law.

The pyramid's sides rise at an angle of 51.5 degrees to the peak, which was originally 481 ft (147 m) above the desert sands

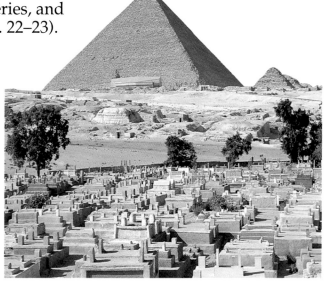

ANCIENT AND MODERN
Giza is now a suburb of the huge modern city of Cairo. This photo shows a Muslim cemetery built next to the Great Pyramid. Khufu's boat museum (p. 29) can be seen against the pyramid. Pollution from cars and factories is damaging the ancient stones. The foundations of the Great Pyramid are shaken every day by the constant flow of buses carrying thousands and thousands of tourists.

HUNDREDS AND THOUSANDS
The Great Pyramid is the largest stone structure ever built. It is impossible to count all the blocks, so the total number can only be guessed at. At the core is an outcrop of rock that was incorporated in the base. The outer casing blocks were so skillfully laid that a knife blade will not slip between them.

AND ON THE INSIDE...
Khufu was probably buried in the King's Chamber, in the heart of his pyramid. This room, lined with shiny red granite, was robbed long ago. But it still contains a sarcophagus, slightly larger than the door. It must have been put there as the pyramid was being built.

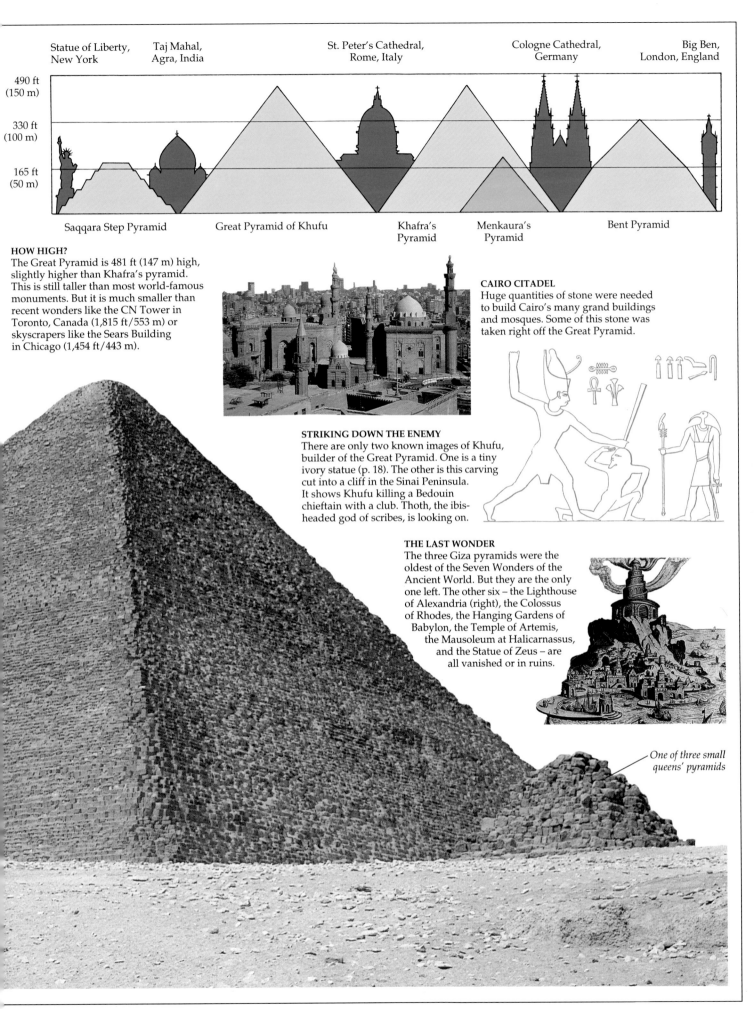

Statue of Liberty, New York

Taj Mahal, Agra, India

St. Peter's Cathedral, Rome, Italy

Cologne Cathedral, Germany

Big Ben, London, England

490 ft (150 m)

330 ft (100 m)

165 ft (50 m)

Saqqara Step Pyramid

Great Pyramid of Khufu

Khafra's Pyramid

Menkaura's Pyramid

Bent Pyramid

HOW HIGH?

The Great Pyramid is 481 ft (147 m) high, slightly higher than Khafra's pyramid. This is still taller than most world-famous monuments. But it is much smaller than recent wonders like the CN Tower in Toronto, Canada (1,815 ft/553 m) or skyscrapers like the Sears Building in Chicago (1,454 ft/443 m).

CAIRO CITADEL

Huge quantities of stone were needed to build Cairo's many grand buildings and mosques. Some of this stone was taken right off the Great Pyramid.

STRIKING DOWN THE ENEMY

There are only two known images of Khufu, builder of the Great Pyramid. One is a tiny ivory statue (p. 18). The other is this carving cut into a cliff in the Sinai Peninsula. It shows Khufu killing a Bedouin chieftain with a club. Thoth, the ibis-headed god of scribes, is looking on.

THE LAST WONDER

The three Giza pyramids were the oldest of the Seven Wonders of the Ancient World. But they are the only one left. The other six – the Lighthouse of Alexandria (right), the Colossus of Rhodes, the Hanging Gardens of Babylon, the Temple of Artemis, the Mausoleum at Halicarnassus, and the Statue of Zeus – are all vanished or in ruins.

One of three small queens' pyramids

Inside the pyramid

WHAT WONDERS ARE HIDDEN inside the pyramids? This question has fascinated people throughout history. The early Christians thought the pharaoh used them to store grain, as the biblical story of Joseph relates. But the pyramids were really royal tombs. Somewhere inside or beneath the huge mass of stone was a burial chamber where the dead king was laid to rest. Since the earliest times, there have been fantastic rumors about the glittering treasures buried with the dead pharaohs. To stop robbers, the pyramid builders hid the entrances and sealed the internal passages with huge plugs of stone. The Middle Kingdom kings created extra passages and false shafts to try and fool robbers. Despite all these efforts, every known pyramid had been looted by 1000 B.C. The few fragments that have been found were overlooked by hasty thieves. The only intact king's burial ever found belonged to Tutankhamun, who had been buried in an underground tomb in the Valley of the Kings. He was lying in three stunning coffins, one made of solid gold, surrounded by priceless treasures. We can only imagine what marvels were buried inside the pyramids.

FORCED ENTRY
The original entrance to the Great Pyramid was concealed by polished casing blocks. Today visitors enter by a lower hole cut by the Arab leader Caliph Ma'mun in the 9th century.

EXPLORING WITHIN
In 1818, the famous Italian adventurer Giovanni Belzoni became the first European to enter Khafra's pyramid at Giza. He was disappointed to find that the burial chamber had been thoroughly robbed. The massive granite sarcophagus was still set into the floor. But there was no trace of the king's body or any treasures.

Two views of French explorers in the Grand Gallery of the Great Pyramid, from the *Description of Egypt*, 1809–1822.

STARS ON THE CEILING
The burial chamber was at the very heart of the pyramid. The sarcophagus often sat at the far end. The roof followed the angle of the pyramid. Unas's pyramid is decorated with stars and hieroglyphs.

Texts from Unas's pyramid

Stars from roof

Painted decoration

The Pyramid Texts

On the inner walls of King Unas's pyramid are the earliest known religious hieroglyphs. These are the Pyramid Texts. Once brightly colored, these magical spells, prayers, and hymns are about the rebirth of the king and his reunion with the gods in the afterlife. They date from about 2340 B.C., which makes them the oldest known religious writings. Later versions of the texts were painted on Middle Kingdom coffins, and on New Kingdom papyruses, in the famous Book of the Dead.

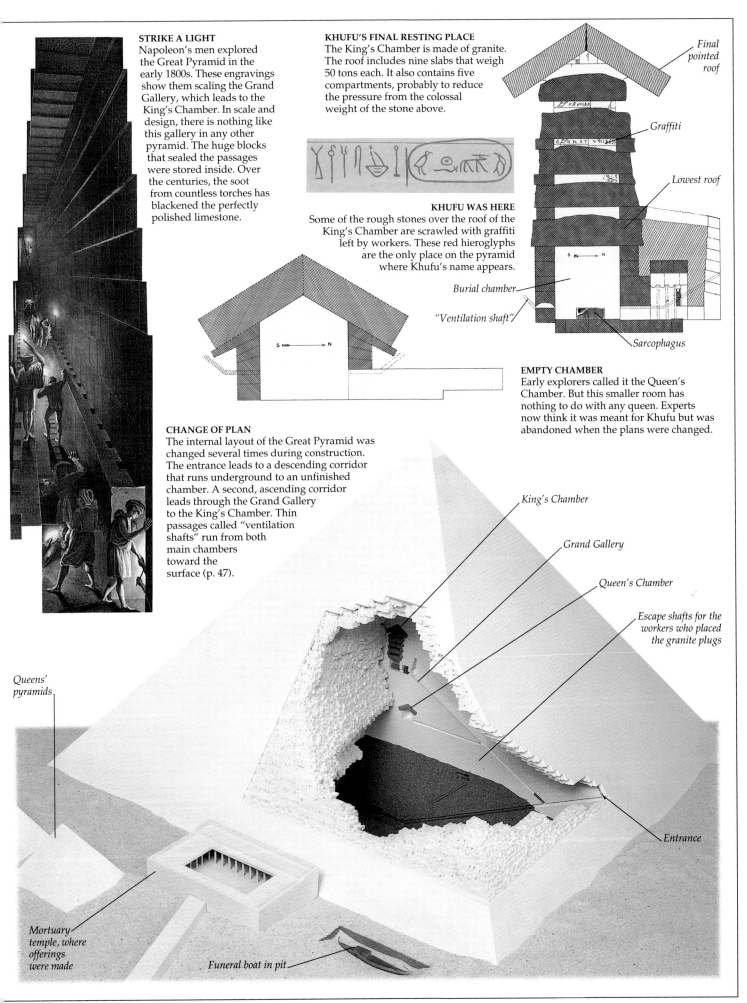

STRIKE A LIGHT
Napoleon's men explored the Great Pyramid in the early 1800s. These engravings show them scaling the Grand Gallery, which leads to the King's Chamber. In scale and design, there is nothing like this gallery in any other pyramid. The huge blocks that sealed the passages were stored inside. Over the centuries, the soot from countless torches has blackened the perfectly polished limestone.

KHUFU'S FINAL RESTING PLACE
The King's Chamber is made of granite. The roof includes nine slabs that weigh 50 tons each. It also contains five compartments, probably to reduce the pressure from the colossal weight of the stone above.

Final pointed roof

Graffiti

Lowest roof

KHUFU WAS HERE
Some of the rough stones over the roof of the King's Chamber are scrawled with graffiti left by workers. These red hieroglyphs are the only place on the pyramid where Khufu's name appears.

Burial chamber

"Ventilation shaft"

Sarcophagus

EMPTY CHAMBER
Early explorers called it the Queen's Chamber. But this smaller room has nothing to do with any queen. Experts now think it was meant for Khufu but was abandoned when the plans were changed.

CHANGE OF PLAN
The internal layout of the Great Pyramid was changed several times during construction. The entrance leads to a descending corridor that runs underground to an unfinished chamber. A second, ascending corridor leads through the Grand Gallery to the King's Chamber. Thin passages called "ventilation shafts" run from both main chambers toward the surface (p. 47).

King's Chamber

Grand Gallery

Queen's Chamber

Escape shafts for the workers who placed the granite plugs

Queens' pyramids

Entrance

Mortuary temple, where offerings were made

Funeral boat in pit

Temples and offerings

A TYPICAL PYRAMID COMPLEX included two temples connected by a long causeway. After the king died, his body was rowed across the Nile to the river or valley temple. Here it was mummified – embalmed, anointed with oils, and wrapped in linen bandages. Seventy days later, when the body was ready, the funeral began. Priests led the procession; women wailed and threw sand into the air. The dead king was carried up the causeway to the mortuary or offering temple. Here the priests performed sacred rites on the mummy before it was laid to rest in the pyramid. After the burial, the pharaoh's spirit would need regular supplies of food and drink. Every day, meals were placed on an altar in the mortuary temple. Before he died, the king would have set aside lands for the maintenance of a community of priests. Their duty was to maintain the temple and provide offerings for the dead king long into the future.

PEEK-A-BOO
This is a statue of Ti, an important official in charge of worship at the pyramid temples of Abusir (pp. 38–39). It was meant as a substitute body that Ti's spirit could inhabit after his death. The statue was placed in a special dark chamber in his tomb called a *serdab*, from the Arabic word for cellar. Ti's face could peer out of a spy hole cut into the tomb wall.

IN THE SHADOW OF THE GREAT PYRAMID
The Great Pyramid was surrounded by a mass of smaller buildings. Khufu's mortuary temple was built on the east side, where the sun was reborn (rose) every day. The dead king hoped to be reborn in the same way. The temple centered around an oblong court with 50 red granite columns. The contrast of white limestone walls, a black basalt floor, and red columns must have been very beautiful. Unfortunately the temple was destroyed long ago. This picture shows the tomb of the nobleman Seshemnufer. Like many important Egyptians, he chose to be buried in the shadow of Khufu's monstrous tomb.

LAND OF PLENTY
The spirits of the dead depended upon the living for their survival in the next world. Tomb pictures often show heaps of bread, beer, fruit, vegetables, and geese piled high on a table. By reciting the formula written beside the picture, the dead person could have a fantastic banquet in the afterlife.

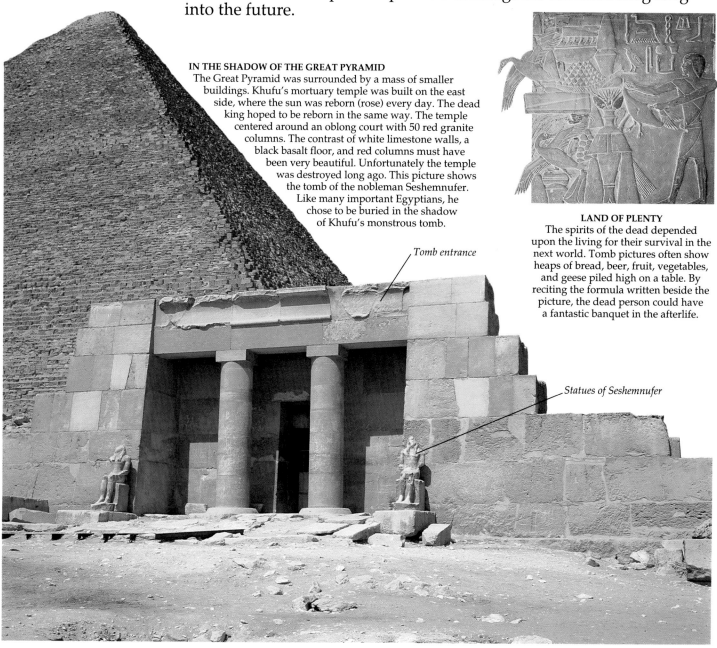

Tomb entrance

Statues of Seshemnufer

MAGIC DOORWAY
Colorful images of food and drink decorate the false door of Prince Merib. If no offerings were left, these magic pictures would come to life.

ESTATE MANAGER
The dead person's family was often pictured on the walls of the tomb. These two young women holding ointment jars are the daughters of Sennedjsui, a treasurer to the king around 2150 B.C. He ran an estate where food for offerings was grown. His titles included "Sole Friend of the King."

ANCIENT BOOKKEEPING
Scribes at the pyramid temple of Neferirkara (p. 38) kept a detailed record of all offerings. These fragments are among the earliest known writings on papyrus. They list daily deliveries of food including meat, bread, and beer.

False doors and stelae

Worshipers came to pray and lay offerings before a stela or false door in the mortuary temple. The stela was a slab of stone inscribed with the dead person's name and titles. In the Old Kingdom, it often took the form of a false door connecting the world of the living with the world of the dead. The door did not open. But the dead person's *ka* (spirit) was thought to pass through it, so he or she could leave the tomb and enjoy a meal in the temple.

Magic hieroglyphs

Falcons represent the high quality of the cloth

The stela would have been set up in the eastern face of Nefertiabet's tomb

Leopard-skin robe

DAILY BREAD
Princess Nefertiabet was buried in a tomb at Giza. She was probably a daughter of one of the pharaohs who built their pyramids there. Her stela shows the princess wearing the leopard-skin robe of a priest. She is seated at a table piled high with loaves of sacred bread. A leg of meat and a headless goose hover above the table. On the right is a list of precious linen to clothe the princess in the afterlife.

The Sphinx

Winged sphinx
made of ivory

FOR MORE THAN 4,500 YEARS, the Sphinx has guarded Khafra's pyramid at Giza. Carved from a huge outcrop of limestone, it is the largest freestanding sculpture to survive from ancient times. It has the body of a lion and the head of a king. The drifting sands have buried it up to the neck for most of its history. Attempts were made to clear it as early as 1400 B.C., by Thutmose IV. When he was a prince, Thutmose fell asleep under the Sphinx's head after a tiring hunt in the desert. In the prince's dream, the Sphinx promised to make him king if he freed it from the suffocating sand. After he had dug the Sphinx out, the prince recorded his dream on a stone tablet between its huge paws.

HEADS LIKE RAMS
In later times, the sphinx became popular as an image of Amun, the most important state god. A long avenue lined with ram-headed sphinxes once linked the great temples of Karnak and Luxor. This pair of bronze sphinxes comes from Nubia (pp. 48–53).

THE SPHINX'S BEARD
This fragment of the Sphinx's beard was found in the sand beneath its head. The beard was probably added a thousand years after the Sphinx was built. Its surface still has traces of its original red coloring. It seems to have been held in place by a column of stone that included a colossal statue of a pharaoh.

BATTERED AND WORN
The Sphinx was carved from an outcrop of rock that was too crumbly to be cut into building blocks for Khafra's pyramid. Its shape probably suggested the form of a lion, onto which Khafra's stonemasons carved an image of their king. The sculpture is about 187 ft (57 m) long and 66 ft (20 m) high. The limestone has been badly weathered over the centuries. The paws were protected with stone facings in Roman times. These were redone recently.

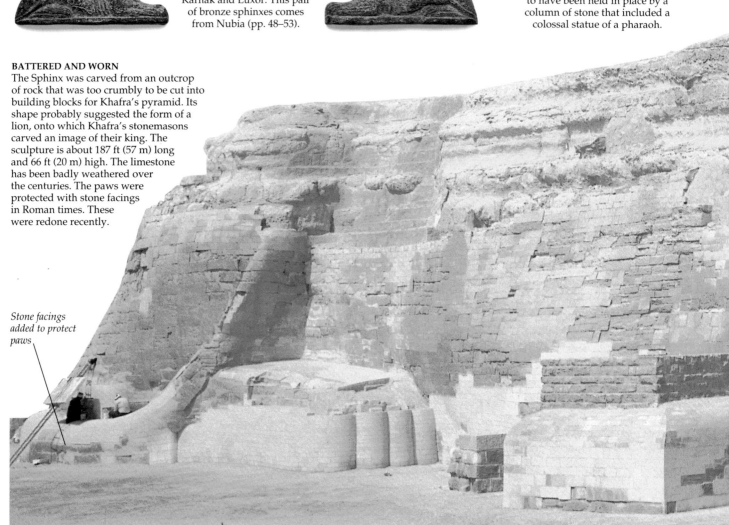

Stone facings
added to protect
paws

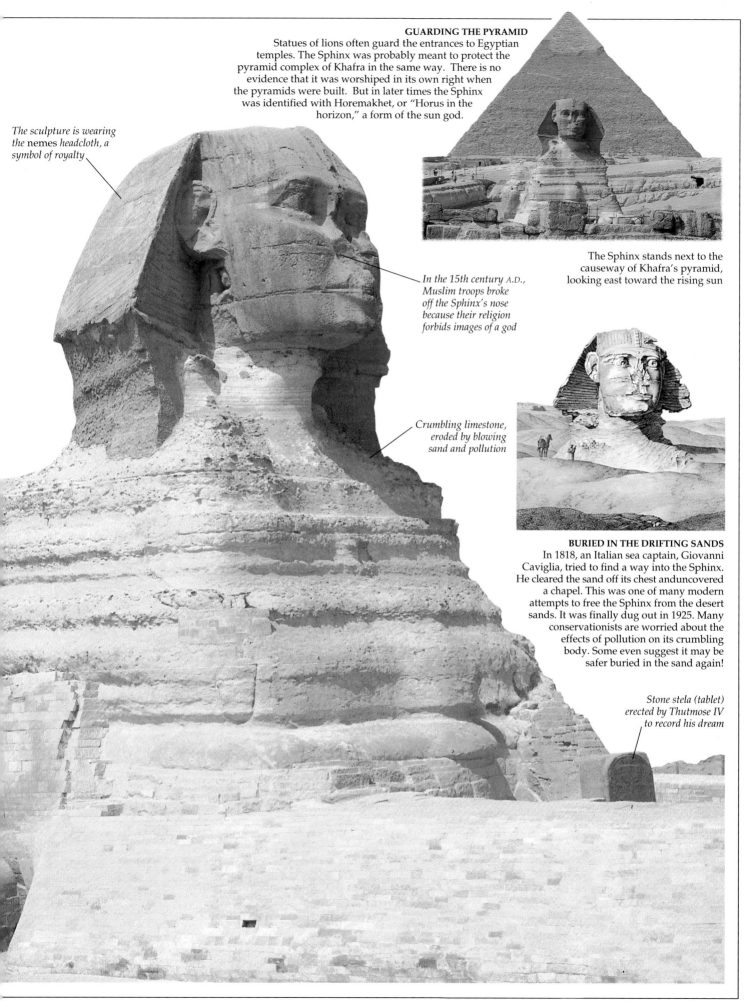

GUARDING THE PYRAMID
Statues of lions often guard the entrances to Egyptian temples. The Sphinx was probably meant to protect the pyramid complex of Khafra in the same way. There is no evidence that it was worshiped in its own right when the pyramids were built. But in later times the Sphinx was identified with Horemakhet, or "Horus in the horizon," a form of the sun god.

The sculpture is wearing the nemes *headcloth, a symbol of royalty*

In the 15th century A.D., *Muslim troops broke off the Sphinx's nose because their religion forbids images of a god*

The Sphinx stands next to the causeway of Khafra's pyramid, looking east toward the rising sun

Crumbling limestone, eroded by blowing sand and pollution

BURIED IN THE DRIFTING SANDS
In 1818, an Italian sea captain, Giovanni Caviglia, tried to find a way into the Sphinx. He cleared the sand off its chest and uncovered a chapel. This was one of many modern attempts to free the Sphinx from the desert sands. It was finally dug out in 1925. Many conservationists are worried about the effects of pollution on its crumbling body. Some even suggest it may be safer buried in the sand again!

Stone stela (tablet) erected by Thutmose IV to record his dream

27

Funeral boats

BOATS WERE THE most important means of transportation for ancient Egyptians. They had no wheeled vehicles or major roads – their only highway was the Nile. In their religion, the Egyptians believed that the sun god Re sailed across the sky in a boat (p. 45). While the pharaoh was alive he traveled the Nile in a beautiful boat, as he took part in state occasions. When he died, the pharaoh needed a boat in the land of the dead. In the Old and Middle Kingdoms, real boats were sometimes buried in pits next to a pharaoh's pyramid. The most famous boat belonged to King Khufu, builder of the Great Pyramid. It is massive – 143 ft (43.5 m) long. In later periods, small models of boats were placed in tombs instead.

SHIP SHAPE
In 1895, two wooden boats were found in a pit near the pyramid of Senusret III (p. 42). Most of the boat pits that have been excavated were empty. The Egyptians may have believed that the dug-out shape provided a magical substitute for a real boat.

3,800-YEAR-OLD OAR
The Egyptians did not have rudders on their boats. Instead they steered with long oars mounted at the stern (back) of the boat. This is a steering oar found with one of the funeral boats of Senusret III. It dates from the Middle Kingdom, around 1850 B.C.

FISHING IN THE NILE MARSHES
This sculpture is in the tomb of Kagemni at Saqqara. It shows men hunting from a reed boat. There are very few trees in the Egyptian desert. So only the best boats were made of wood, which had to be imported from Lebanon. Others were made from bundles of reeds tied tightly together.

Flame

Incense burner

Attendants

Mummified body of dead man or woman

Boat's prow, shaped like a bundle of papyrus reeds

Eye of Horus, a symbol of protection and rebirth

Sealed storage jar for voyage

A FUNERAL PROCESSION

The Book of the Dead is a series of spells to help a dead person's soul in the journey through the afterlife. This detail from the book by the scribe Hunefer shows a funeral procession. The mummy of Hunefer is carried in a boat mounted on a sled and pulled by priests. At the front of the procession, mourners wail and throw sand in the air.

Khufu's funeral boat

In 1954, an Egyptian archeologist made a remarkable discovery. Just south of the Great Pyramid of Giza, he discovered a boat pit sealed for over 4,500 years. Under massive slabs of limestone lay 651 pieces of carved timber. These were put together to make an elegant boat. The name of King Khufu, builder of the Great Pyramid, was written on some of the pieces. It must have been buried by his successor, Radjedef, right after Khufu's death.

Khufu's boat on display in a museum next to the Great Pyramid

Prow shaped like bundle of reeds

Five pairs of oars

Canopy

The royal cabin

Stern

Steering oar

Model of Khufu's funeral boat

BOAT BENEATH THE PYRAMID

Khufu's boat had been dismantled to fit it into the pit. Luckily the builders had made notations such as "fore" and "aft" on some of the pieces. These clues helped the team who rebuilt the boat 4,500 years later. Tests on the wood show the boat was used at least once. This may have been while Khufu was alive, or to carry his body to the pyramid tomb during his funeral.

Canopy to protect crew and mummy from hot sun

Falcon heads

Steering oars

Steersman crouching at stern

Stern of carved wood shaped like a bundle of papyrus reeds

Priest with shaved head

Papyrus leaf decoration painted on blades

FUNERAL BOAT OF THE MIDDLE KINGDOM

This model boat is carrying a mummy on a pilgrimage to Abydos. This sacred city was the center of worship for the god Osiris, who was thought to have risen from the dead. All Egyptians hoped that their mummy would follow Osiris's example. The boat probably dates from the Middle Kingdom, 2040–1750 B.C. At that time, small wooden boats were often placed in tombs, along with numerous objects, such as food, makeup, and furniture, that the dead person would need in the afterlife.

Planning the pyramid

THE PYRAMIDS REQUIRED careful planning. First a site had to be chosen. For religious reasons, this was always on the west bank of the Nile, where the sun set. It had to be close to the river, because the stone would arrive by boat, but well above flood level. The pyramid also required a solid base of rock that would not crack under its enormous weight. Then the site was leveled and true north was calculated, so the sides could be lined up with the four compass points. The Egyptians probably did this by using the stars, since they did not have magnetic compasses. They had set squares and special tools like the *merkhet* to help in their calculations.

Pegging the foundations

DIVINE PROPORTIONS
Like sculpture and painting, pyramid building followed a fixed system of proportion. Artists' models like this one show that the Egyptians drew a grid of horizontal and vertical lines to calculate what they called "divine proportions." They used small models or sketches to plan large works. Two small limestone models of pyramids have been found. But there is no way of knowing if these were made before or after the pyramids.

LEVEL PEGGING
This ancient cord on a peg is probably one of a pair used to mark out the foundations of a building. The southeast corner of the Great Pyramid is only 0.5 in (1.3 cm) higher than the northwest corner. This incredible accuracy was achieved by digging trenches, filling them with water, and marking the level. Then all the rock above the line was hacked away until the foundation was perfectly flat.

Wooden peg

Cord made from the flax plant

GUARANTEEING A TIGHT FIT
Egyptian masons (stonecutters) had tools called boning rods to make the stone blocks perfectly smooth. This scene from the tomb of the official Rekhmire (c. 1450 B.C.) shows how these were used. The masons are holding the rods at right angles to the stone so the string is stretched tight. Any bumps are chiseled smooth.

Pair of boning rods

BREAKING THE RULES
The basic unit of measurement was the cubit, the length from the elbow to the tip of the thumb. This was equal to 20.62 in (52.4 cm). The wooden rod below is marked in cubits, palms, and digits. There were four digits in a palm, and seven palms in a cubit. The Egyptians also buried ritual cubit rods during foundation ceremonies.

Fragment from a ritual cubit rod made of schist

PYRAMID CALCULATIONS
This is part of the Rhind Papyrus, written about 1550 B.C. It shows a series of problems about the relationship between the angle of a pyramid and its overall dimensions. The angle of the sloping sides is called the *seked*. It is equal to half the width of the base, divided by the pyramid's height and multiplied by seven.

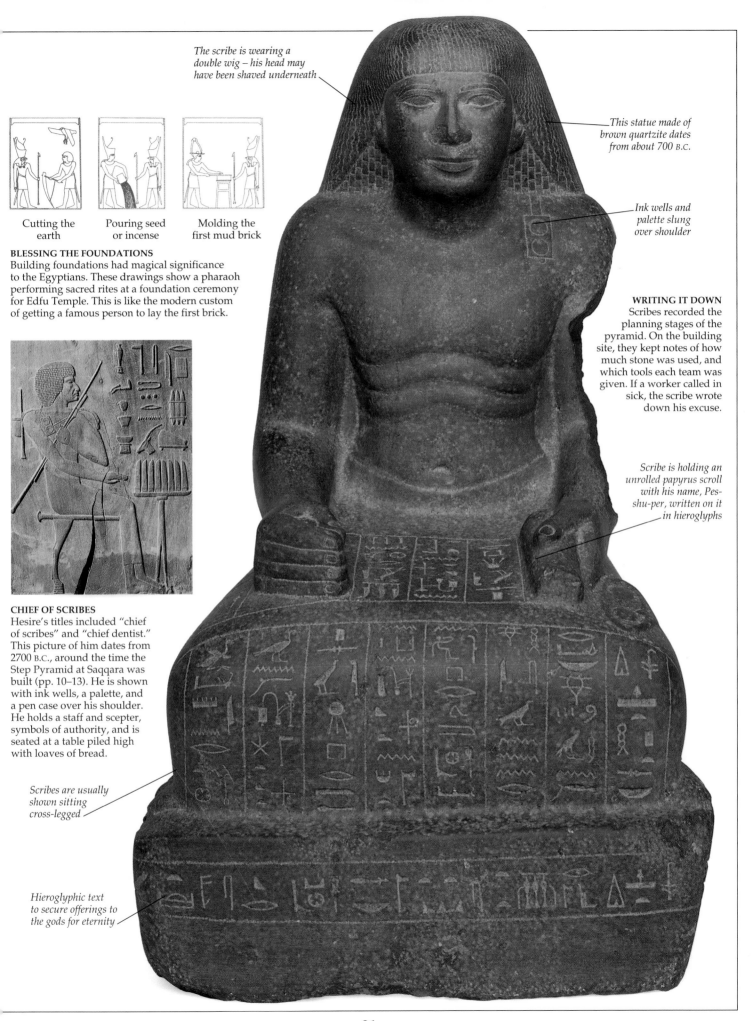

The scribe is wearing a double wig – his head may have been shaved underneath

This statue made of brown quartzite dates from about 700 B.C.

Ink wells and palette slung over shoulder

Cutting the earth

Pouring seed or incense

Molding the first mud brick

BLESSING THE FOUNDATIONS
Building foundations had magical significance to the Egyptians. These drawings show a pharaoh performing sacred rites at a foundation ceremony for Edfu Temple. This is like the modern custom of getting a famous person to lay the first brick.

WRITING IT DOWN
Scribes recorded the planning stages of the pyramid. On the building site, they kept notes of how much stone was used, and which tools each team was given. If a worker called in sick, the scribe wrote down his excuse.

Scribe is holding an unrolled papyrus scroll with his name, Pes-shu-per, written on it in hieroglyphs

CHIEF OF SCRIBES
Hesire's titles included "chief of scribes" and "chief dentist." This picture of him dates from 2700 B.C., around the time the Step Pyramid at Saqqara was built (pp. 10–13). He is shown with ink wells, a palette, and a pen case over his shoulder. He holds a staff and scepter, symbols of authority, and is seated at a table piled high with loaves of bread.

Scribes are usually shown sitting cross-legged

Hieroglyphic text to secure offerings to the gods for eternity

Building in brick and stone

IT TOOK HUNDREDS OF THOUSANDS of pieces of stone to build a pyramid. The Great Pyramid is made of about 2,300,000 blocks, each weighing an average of 2.5 tons. The largest slabs, in the roof of the King's Chamber, weigh 50 tons. Quarrying all this stone and moving it to the site was an awesome task. The core of the pyramid was made from local limestone, a fairly soft rock. But the high-quality limestone used for the outer casing came from Tura, across the Nile. Some internal chambers and passages were made of granite, a harder stone that came from Aswan, 500 miles (800 km) upriver. All year round, gangs of workers at the quarries cut rough stone blocks out of the ground. When the river flooded and rose closer to the quarries, the stone blocks were loaded onto boats and carried to the pyramid site. The teams even wrote their names on the stones – some blocks in the Meidum Pyramid (p. 14) are labeled "Enduring Gang," "Vigorous Gang," or "Boat Gang."

BASALT
This hard black stone could be highly polished. This quality made it popular for sarcophagi, sculpture, and monumental inscriptions like the Rosetta Stone.

Both cartouches (hieroglyphic names) of Ramses II, who ruled from 1279 to 1213 B.C.

SANDSTONE
Harder than limestone but softer than granite, sandstone was used for building and sculpture. This is a foundation deposit (p. 50) from the temple of Ptah at Memphis.

GRANITE
This hard, heavy stone was used for sculpture and sarcophagi (stone coffins) and sometimes for lining passages and chambers inside pyramids. It was very difficult to quarry. An unfinished obelisk (stone pillar) is still lying in the Aswan quarry. It weighs over 1,000 tons and would have stood about 100 ft (30 m) tall.

ROWING STONES
Quarries and pyramids were close to the Nile, so the stone could be transported by boat. This carving from the tomb of the official Ipi shows a cargo boat carrying a huge block of stone. The sail is rolled up, so the boat is probably cruising downstream (northward) with the current.

RESTORATION PROJECT
The best Tura limestone was saved for the pyramid's outer casing. Most of these "casing blocks" were stripped away by later builders who were too lazy to quarry their own. This block shows the original angle of the pyramid of Unas at Saqqara, c. 2340 B.C., which has collapsed into a heap of rubble. More than a thousand years after it was built, Khaemwaset, Ramses II's son, tried to restore it by refitting the fallen casing blocks.

LIMESTONE
Old Kingdom pyramids were mostly made of limestone. Because papyrus – the ancient Egyptians' paper – was so expensive, sketches and rough notes were often done on fragments of pottery or limestone. These are called ostraca. This ostracon has a sketch of the god Osiris.

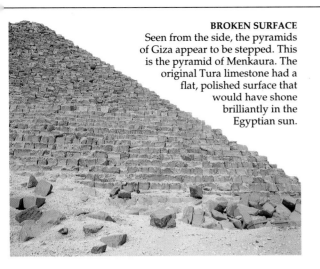

BRICKMAKERS AT WORK
This painting from the tomb of Rekhmire at Thebes, c. 1450 B.C., shows workers mixing and molding mud bricks.

Straw and sand keep the brick from cracking when it dries

Cartouche

1752

ROYAL STAMP
Mud bricks were often stamped with the name of the pharaoh. This wooden stamp has the cartouche of King Amenhotep II, c. 1400 B.C.

Mud bricks

These were the most common building material in ancient Egypt. Middle Kingdom pyramids were made of mud bricks with only an outer facing of limestone. Today mud bricks are still made by the same process used by the ancients. Wet Nile mud is mixed with straw and sand and pushed into a wooden mold. Then the soft bricks are set out to dry in the burning sun. The Egyptian word for brick, *tobe*, is the origin of the modern word *adobe*, a kind of brick architecture.

Mud brick from Thebes, c. 1000 B.C.

A worker leaves rows of bricks to dry in the sun, in this picture from the tomb of Rekhmire

33

Tools for building

ROCK DRILL
This curved flake of flint is an Egyptian tool from the Pyramid Age. It looks too fragile to work stone. But attached to a wooden pole and spun vigorously with a bow, it became a powerful drill. For a smoother cut, the drill would be used with sand or crushed quartz, mixed with water or a little olive oil.

ALL AROUND THE GREAT temples, tombs, and pyramids, Egyptologists have found tools left by builders and sculptors. Some of these were lost or broken on the site. But others were left there for religious reasons. The Egyptians believed that a sacred building, such as a temple or pyramid, had a spirit that would have to be repaired in the next world. So the workers left tools for their spirits to use after they died. The design of these tools has changed little over the centuries. It is amazing what wonders the builders created with such simple implements.

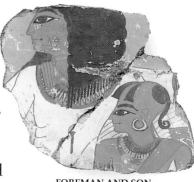

FOREMAN AND SON
Tools were precious. They were often issued each morning by a foreman, who organized his team of workers and locked the tools away at night. This painting shows Anherkhau, a foreman who worked in the Valley of the Kings, with his son. It dates from 1150 B.C.

HIGHER AND HIGHER
Ancient paintings show that the Egyptians built scaffolding. This detail from the tomb of Rekhmire, c. 1450 B.C., shows workers putting the final touches on a statue of the pharaoh. They are standing on a network of light poles lashed together with knots of plant rope.

POLISHING IT UP
After a block of stone had been roughly cut and shaped, it might be burnished (rubbed down with a smooth stone) to give it a polished surface.

MASON'S MALLET
For thousands of years, masons all over the world have hit their chisels with mallets (wooden hammers). This one is made of very hard wood.

Copper

Bronze

HARD ROCK
Most stones are too hard to be worked with copper tools. Instead they were quarried with pieces of dolerite, a very hard rock. This pounder is made of softer granite.

CHISELS
Masons work stone with chisels. These bronze and copper chisels were used to create fine details. The tips could be heated to make them cut better.

Wide "dovetail" end was pushed into a recess in the stone and stuck there with plaster or mortar

BUTTERFLY CLAMP
Clamps were used to hold blocks of stone together. The wide ends were plastered into holes in the two stones. Many clamps are inscribed with the cartouche (name) of the royal builder.

GETTING THE AXE

Axes were used as weapons of war all over the ancient world. They were also good for chopping wood, or to show the owner's power. This ceremonial axe was found in the foundations of a temple.

Hieroglyphs with cartouche of the pharaoh Thutmose III, who ruled from 1479 to 1425 B.C.

Furniture maker hitting a chisel with a wooden mallet

FOR CUTTING (NOT SHAVING)

The adze was an ancient carpenter's favorite tool. Many paintings show workers chopping and planing wood with adzes. This one from c. 1400 B.C. is unusual because the carpenter is unshaven with scruffy hair. Egyptians are almost always shown with perfect hair and makeup.

Model adze with wooden handle and copper blade

Wooden model of a curved knife

Model saw with wooden handle and copper blade

Magic tool kit

This axe, adze, chisel, knife, and saw were all found in the foundations of Thutmose III's temple at Deir el-Bahri (p. 41). They are models, not real tools, and must have been put there by the workers in a special ceremony.

Model chisel

Worker cutting with knife-like saw, from tomb of Rekhmire, c. 1450 B.C.

Wood was very rare in the desert and often had to be imported from Lebanon

Tang, a projection that fitted into the wooden handle

Tip is curved up so it will not catch

PULL (DON'T PUSH)

Unlike a modern saw, this ancient tool was designed to cut as the worker pulled it toward his or her body. Its wooden handle has long since rotted away.

Cutting edge

Blunt edge that rubbed against wood but did not cut

The pyramid rises

N<small>O RECORDS SURVIVE</small> to tell us how the pyramids were built. The only ancient account, by the Greek historian Herodotus, was written 2,000 years later and cannot be trusted. He claimed that gangs of 100,000 workmen toiled for 20 years to build the Great Pyramid. We now believe that about 4,000 skilled laborers worked all year round. During *Akhet*, the yearly flood, thousands of peasants left their flooded fields and came to help on the site. There are many theories about how the heavy blocks of stone were lifted into place. Herodotus said they used lifting machines, but there is no evidence for this. It seems more likely that the stones were dragged up a ramp that grew as the pyramid rose. Once the capstone was in place, the ramp was dismantled.

MUD-BRICK RAMP
Remains of ramps have been found near several pyramids. This detailed drawing is from the tomb of Rekhmire, made 1,000 years after the Great Pyramid. It shows a building block lying on a ramp.

Polished casing was probably white

TWO-WAY TRAFFIC
The ramp was probably strictly organized into up and down lanes. One lane – in this model, the far left lane – is being raised, and is closed to traffic.

Side of ramp being raised *Stones going up* *Empty sleds coming down* *Stacks of blocks ready to be hauled up ramp*

BUILDING A TRUE PYRAMID
This model shows the most popular theory – the use of one long supply ramp. As the pyramid grew higher, the ramp was increased in height and length. The top of the pyramid was a great square platform ready to receive the next layer of stones. In the model, the fine outer casing stones are being added as each layer is finished. But some experts argue that the whole pyramid was cased from the top down as the last stage of construction. The boat is delivering logs for use in ramps, rollers, and scaffolding.

The ramp was narrow, and was always kept at a gentle angle

Teams of men, at least 30 per sled, pull stones up ramp

BIG DRAG

Wooden sleds with runners were the best way of moving heavy loads. Sleds are quite common in Egyptian art, and several real sleds have been found. This papyrus painting (c. 1000 B.C.) shows a funeral procession. Men are dragging the coffin, which is covered by a canopy and mounted on a sled. When moving stones, the workers probably laid logs across the ramp to stop the heavy sleds from getting bogged down in the mud.

UPWARD SPIRAL

Some experts have proposed that the stones were dragged up a system of spiral ramps winding around the pyramid. The ramps could have stood either on the casing blocks, or on separate foundations in front of the pyramid. But it would have been virtually impossible to turn the stones around the corners. Spiral ramps would also obscure the whole pyramid, which would make measurements difficult. Making sure the four sides came to a perfect point would have required constant measuring.

CRACK THE WHIP

Drawings and films about ancient Egypt often show sweating slaves being driven on by bosses with whips. This is totally untrue. The hard labor was done by peasant-farmers. They believed their pharaoh was a god and were probably happy to help him achieve everlasting life.

Workers add to height of ramp

A team dragging a block of stone arrives at the top

Awnings to shelter foremen and supplies of food and water

Fine white Tura limestone for outer casing

Stockpile of local limestone for core

Teams work on scaffolding to fit the final casing stones on each layer

Work in progress on entrance to internal passages in north face of pyramid

As the wall gets higher, the workers use wooden pole scaffolding

Teams of workmen build the square enclosure wall that will encircle the pyramid

A slow decline

THE KINGS OF EGYPT'S fifth and sixth dynasties continued the tradition of pyramid building. But their pyramids were smaller and not as well built. The largest, made for King Neferirkara at Abusir, is about the same size as Menkaura's pyramid, the smallest of the Giza trio. The kings still cased their pyramids in fine Tura limestone. But underneath was a core of small, roughly joined stones. These have slowly collapsed, so that little more than piles of rubble remain. The cult of the sun god increased during this period, and many sun temples were built. These magnificent buildings were places of worship. Food offerings were also collected here before being taken by boat and placed in nearby pyramid temples.

EASY ACCESS
The fifth- and sixth-dynasty kings did not make much effort to conceal the entrances to their pyramids. This made it easy for tomb robbers to get in. This drawing shows the entrance to Nyuserra's pyramid at Abusir. It comes from Howard Vyse's famous book *The Pyramids of Gizeh,* published in 1837.

MAGIC HIEROGLYPHS
Magic spells were essential to guarantee the king's survival in the afterlife. These hieroglyphs from the pyramid temple of King Sahura display his many royal titles.

FIFTH-DYNASTY PYRAMID COMPLEX
Four kings built their pyramids at Abusir, just south of Giza. This reconstruction shows, from left to right, the pyramids of Neferirkara, Nyuserra, and Sahura. Beyond them are the sun temples of Userkaf and Nyuserra. The causeway (raised approach) to Nyuserra's pyramid takes a sharp turn, because it was originally meant to lead to the pyramid of the earlier king Neferirkara. After his death, the king was mummified in or around the river temple. Then his mummy was carried up the causeway, and sacred rites were performed in the pyramid temple. Finally the dead king was laid to rest inside the burial chamber beneath the pyramid.

Falcon

The king is holding the divine mace, a weapon and symbol of royal power

LEGLESS NEAR GIZA
Czech archeologists identified the ruined pyramid of Raneferef in 1982. It is in Abusir and dates from about 2400 B.C. This beautiful statue of the king was found in his mortuary temple. Behind his head is a falcon, a symbol of royalty and the god Horus. It clasps *shenu* rings, which symbolize eternity, in its claws. The king was once sitting down, but his legs have been broken off.

Statue is carved from pink limestone

The top of the king's kilt

ENDURANCE TEST
Despite its name, "The places of Nyuserra are enduring," this pyramid is just a pile of sand and rubble.

Deshret *crown, worn by pharaohs and the goddess Neith*

Faint mustache, *which suggests that the subject is a man*

The statue is made *of green schist, a hard, shiny rock*

BEARING GIFTS
A long procession of elegant figures lines the funerary temple of King Sahura. They have come to pay their respects to the dead pharaoh and place offerings in his temple.

Carved papyrus buds

Carved palm leaves

PAPYRUS COLUMN
The columns in Sahura's mortuary temple were made of solid granite 12 ft (3.7 m) high. Each one is carved like a bundle of papyrus stems with the capital (top) shaped like papyrus buds.

Papyrus stems tied together

Sahura's royal names and titles

Cross section of a papyrus column

PALM COLUMN
Sahura's valley temple had eight columns carved to look like palm trees. They were inscribed with hieroglyphs highlighted with green paste.

MYSTERIOUS PORTRAIT
An interesting legend about the beginning of the fifth dynasty is mentioned in a papyrus in the Berlin Museum. In the story, the wife of a priest has three children with the sun god Re. Many gods and goddesses come to the birth, and the goddess Isis gives names to the three "Sons of Re." They were Userkaf, Sahura, and Neferirkara, the first three kings of the fifth dynasty. Userkaf built his pyramid at Saqqara. This elegant statue was found in the ruins of his sun temple, near Abusir. Since statues of kings usually have beards, some experts think it may represent the goddess Neith. But the faint mustache and the statue's location suggest that it is a royal portrait of Userkaf.

BACK TO SAQQARA
Pepy I was a sixth-dynasty pharaoh. He is famous for an unusual, life-sized statue made of copper. This portrait by Winifred Brunton (pp. 42–43) is based on it. Like most fifth- and sixth-dynasty kings, Pepy I built his pyramid at Saqqara. He called it "Pepy is established and beautiful." The last sixth-dynasty king, Pepy II, ruled for 94 years, longer than any other pharaoh. After his death, around 2181 B.C., the Old Kingdom collapsed. It would be more than 200 years before another true pyramid was built.

The Middle Kingdom revival

AFTER A LONG PERIOD OF DISORDER and civil war, Egypt was reunited around 2040 B.C. The period that followed is known as the Middle Kingdom. Strong kings expanded the empire and revived the tradition of pyramid building. They were inspired by the great pyramids of the Old Kingdom and often built their tombs near the old sites. But the Middle Kingdom pyramids do not have the same grandeur. They were usually based around a core of mud bricks, many of which slowly collapsed over the years. Middle Kingdom pharaohs were preoccupied with creating complicated devices and false passages to keep thieves from finding their burial chambers. But the kings were buried with priceless treasures, and the robbers stopped at nothing. Despite the elaborate precautions, all the pyramids were robbed in the period of unrest that followed the end of the Middle Kingdom, around 1750 B.C.

Red crown of Lower Egypt

Statue is made of 16 pieces of carefully jointed cedar wood

Long scepter in the shape of a shepherd's crook

Short kilt

SENUSRET II
The cartouche (hieroglyphic name) of Senusret II can be seen on this colorful piece of gold jewelry. It was part of a treasure found in the tomb of the princess Sat-Hathor III at Dahshur. Senusret II built his pyramid at El Lahun, near the Faiyum oasis.

STRIDING KING
Amenemhat I was the first Middle Kingdom king to have a true pyramid. He built it at Lisht, and called it "Amenemhat is high and beautiful." His son, Senusret I, also chose to be buried at Lisht. This is one of two statues of Senusret I found near his pyramid. He is wearing the red crown of Lower Egypt; the other figure wears the white crown of Upper Egypt. Around his pyramid were 10 smaller pyramids where his favorite queens and daughters were buried.

Wall of whole pyramid enclosure

Rubble

Western side of pyramid

King's burial chamber

Shaft tombs

Entrance

SECRET ENTRANCE
This is a plan of Amenemhat III's first pyramid, at Dahshur (pp. 42–43). It had a concealed entrance and a maze of passages and false doors. Recent excavations have revealed even more inner rooms.

Great temple at Deir el-Bahri

The first pharaoh of the Middle Kingdom, Nebhepetra Mentuhotep, was one of Egypt's greatest rulers. During his 51 years on the throne, art and architecture began to prosper again. Mentuhotep chose a bay in the cliffs at Deir el-Bahri, near Thebes, for his funerary temple. This unusual complex had colonnades, a ramp, and rows of statues and trees. High on a terrace were six shrines with shafts leading to the tombs of the king's wives and daughters. There were two more tombs beneath the temple, but Mentuhotep's mummy or coffin was not found in either one. The whole complex is badly preserved. It has been overshadowed by a similar, larger temple built 500 years later by Queen Hatshepsut.

HOLY OF HOLIES
In her own era, Hatshepsut was famous for her radiant beauty. The ancient Egyptians called her temple Djeseru-Djeseru, "Holy of Holies."

QUEEN WITH A BEARD
Hatshepsut was one of the few women to be crowned pharaoh of Egypt. To strengthen her claim to the throne, she had herself portrayed as the daughter of the god Amun. This scene from the Karnak temple shows her running in the royal *sed* course (pp. 12–13). She is wearing a false beard, a sign of royalty.

PYRAMID OR MASTABA?
Was Mentuhotep's temple capped with a stone pyramid? Until recently, most experts thought so. But a new study has suggested that the top story may have been a flat-topped mastaba.

Mentuhotep's temple, with a pyramid

Red crown of Lower Egypt

Cobras, thought to protect the pharaoh by spitting fire at enemies

False beard, worn by the pharaoh on important occasions

EMBRACED BY A GODDESS
Mentuhotep reigned from 2055 to 2004 B.C. As a young king he reunited the two lands – Lower and Upper Egypt – and won many victories over the Nubians and Libyans. But unlike the great kings of the Old Kingdom, he did not make Memphis his capital. Instead he ruled from Thebes in the south (p. 8). In this fine fragment from Deir el-Bahri, he is shown being embraced by the hands of a goddess.

COLORED RELIEF
The walls of Mentuhotep's temple at Deir el-Bahri were lined with colorful paintings. Thousands of broken fragments have been found in the ruins. They are now in museums all over the world. This fragment showing a man, probably an offering bearer, is in the Bolton Museum in England.

Continued on next page

FALCON PENDANT
This pendant is made of gold inlaid with the red stone carnelian. It is part of several magnificent treasures of jewelry found around the Middle Kingdom pyramids at Dahshur and El Lahun.

Senusret III

This great pharaoh reigned from 1874 to 1855 B.C. He created a strong, centralized government and conquered Nubia to the south. He built his pyramid at Dahshur. The design of the pyramid buildings and the king's sarcophagus was influenced by Djoser's Step Pyramid complex (pp. 10–13), built 800 years earlier.

Large ears, a feature of many statues of this period

Royal nemes headcloth

THE BLACK PYRAMID
Senusret III and his successor Amenemhat III built their pyramids at Dahshur, just south of Saqqara. This is Amenemhat III's pyramid, often called the Black Pyramid. The corridors and chambers, including the tombs of at least three queens, were dug about 40 ft (12 m) underground. But the king's burial chamber, with its beautiful granite sarcophagus, was never used. Like most Middle Kingdom pyramids, the Black Pyramid is now just a pile of rubble. The core of mud bricks has collapsed over the centuries, and the fine stone facings were plundered for later building projects.

PHARAOH'S FEATURES
This is Senusret III as he may have looked in life. It is one of a series of reconstructions of famous Egyptians painted by Winifred Brunton, based on careful observations of ancient statues.

The vulture goddess Nekhbet

Cartouche of Senusret III

LOOKING HIS AGE
Senusret III looks stern and thoughtful in this statue carved from black granite. This new, more realistic style of portraiture was introduced during his reign.

Belt buckle with cartouche of Senusret III

Pleated kilt known as a shendyt kilt

A PRINCESS'S TREASURE
This beautiful piece of jewelry was found in the tomb of princess Mereret near the pyramid of Senusret III. One of the king's victories is symbolized by sphinxes trampling on Nubians.

Brick
arch

Slabs of
limestone

Roof of chamber

Sarcophagus

THE SECOND PYRAMID
Amenemhat III built his second
pyramid at Hawara. His architects
built an amazing series of devices
to baffle robbers – deep wells, blind
corridors, secret trapdoors, and
passages sealed with mighty stone
slabs. This is his burial chamber,
which is covered by limestone
blocks weighing 50 tons each.
Thieves still broke in, stealing
all the king's treasures and
burning his body.

Reconstruction painting of
Amenemhat III, by Winifred
Brunton, done in the 1920s

MIGHTY HEAD
The eyes have been
gouged out of this massive
head of Amenemhat III. Carved
in black granite, it was once
part of a full-length statue.

Amenemhat III

The grandson of Senusret III, Amenemhat III was
one of the most powerful pharaohs ever to rule Egypt.
He built two pyramids and a famous labyrinth (maze)
said to contain 3,000 rooms. He is also credited with
building an impressive irrigation network. It was an
ancient forerunner of the Aswan Dam, with massive
dikes and sluices to control the water level of the Nile.

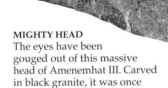

CAPSTONE
In the rubble around the
Dahshur pyramid, a granite
capstone was found. It is
carved with Amenemhat III's
royal titles and prayers to the
sun god. The hieroglyphs on
this detail read "Seeing the
beauty of Re." Why wasn't
Amenemhat buried in the
Dahshur pyramid? He may
have built it as a cenotaph, a
symbolic place for his spirit to
dwell. Or he may have decided
that the layout wasn't complex
enough to fool robbers.

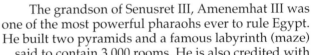

LORD OF ALL LANDS
Another piece of gold jewelry from Princess
Mereret's tomb. Near Amenemhat III's name
are hieroglyphs that read, "The good god,
lord of all lands and foreign countries."

Pyramidions

THE MASSIVE ROYAL PYRAMIDS of old inspired private individuals to build pyramid-shaped tombs in the New Kingdom. These were small brick buildings with pointed roofs capped by a pyramidion, or capstone. They were often whitewashed and had stelae, stone tablets, on the front. Prayers to the sun god Re were inscribed on the stelae and pyramidions. A courtyard often stood in front of the tomb. This served as a chapel where worshipers could place offerings and pray. An underground passage led to a vaulted burial chamber where the mummy lay. Hundreds of these small pyramids were built on the west bank of the Nile by officials, scribes, and the artisans who worked on the great royal tombs of the New Kingdom.

A PRAYER TO THE SUN GOD
This very pointy pyramidion is made of white limestone. Like most pyramidions, it stands about 2 ft (60 cm) tall. It is inscribed with prayers to the sun god Re from its owner, Bugentef, who is standing in a niche wearing a wig and an apron. The steep sides are unusual, and are similar to the later pyramids from Meroe in the Sudan (pp. 48–53).

The hieroglyphic inscription reads, "An offering that the King gives to Re-Horakhty-Atum (sun god), lord of the two lands of Heliopolis, that he may give all offerings good and pure to the Ka (body) of the servant of the sun Bugentef"

UNKNOWN OWNER
There are no hieroglyphic inscriptions on this limestone pyramidion, so we do not know who it was made for. Two of its sides have carvings of the dead person kneeling with hands raised in prayer before an imaginary doorway. This is like the Old Kingdom false door (p. 25) that linked this world to the next.

Carving of dead person praying

Priests   *Mummy*   *Stela*   *Pyramidion*   *Mud-brick pyramid*

A PYRAMIDION ON PAPYRUS
This painting shows a funeral ceremony taking place before a tomb capped with a pyramidion. It is a detail from the Book of the Dead, that describes the journey of the soul in the afterlife. The ceremony shown here is the "Opening of the Mouth" performed on the mummy of Hunefer (p. 29).

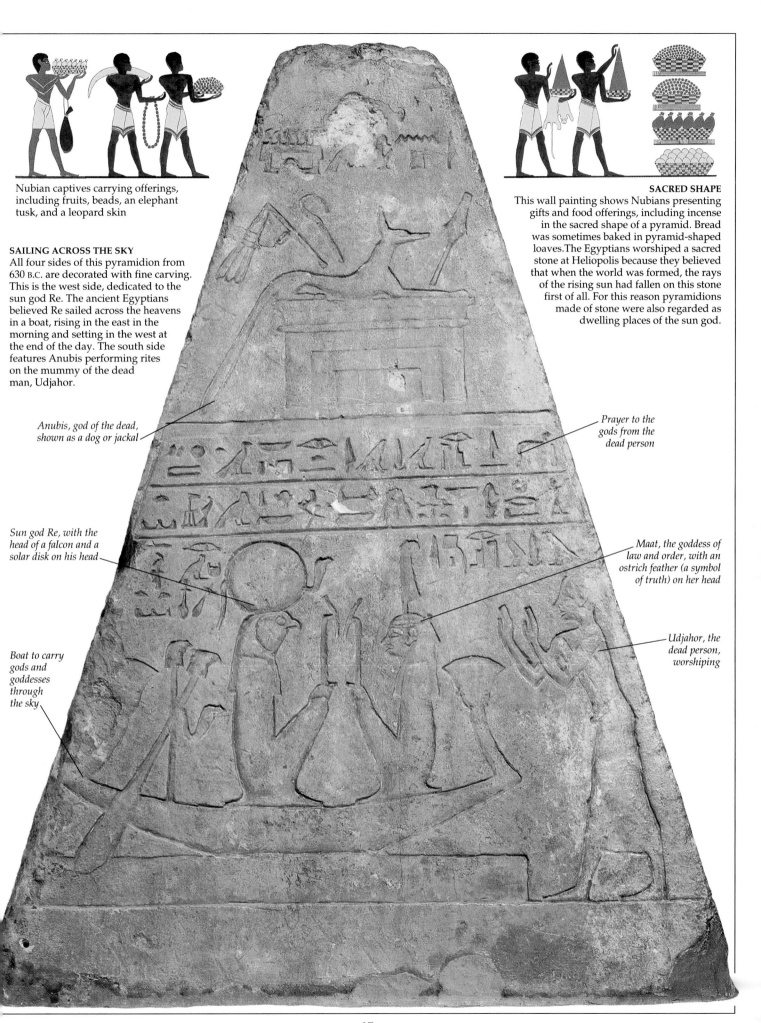

Nubian captives carrying offerings, including fruits, beads, an elephant tusk, and a leopard skin

SAILING ACROSS THE SKY
All four sides of this pyramidion from 630 B.C. are decorated with fine carving. This is the west side, dedicated to the sun god Re. The ancient Egyptians believed Re sailed across the heavens in a boat, rising in the east in the morning and setting in the west at the end of the day. The south side features Anubis performing rites on the mummy of the dead man, Udjahor.

Anubis, god of the dead, shown as a dog or jackal

Sun god Re, with the head of a falcon and a solar disk on his head

Boat to carry gods and goddesses through the sky

SACRED SHAPE
This wall painting shows Nubians presenting gifts and food offerings, including incense in the sacred shape of a pyramid. Bread was sometimes baked in pyramid-shaped loaves. The Egyptians worshiped a sacred stone at Heliopolis because they believed that when the world was formed, the rays of the rising sun had fallen on this stone first of all. For this reason pyramidions made of stone were also regarded as dwelling places of the sun god.

Prayer to the gods from the dead person

Maat, the goddess of law and order, with an ostrich feather (a symbol of truth) on her head

Udjahor, the dead person, worshiping

Riddles of the pyramids

CONSIDERING THEY WERE BUILT 4,500 years ago, we know a surprising amount about the Egyptian pyramids. But many mysteries remain. Almost everything we know, we learned in the last two centuries. A great breakthrough was made in 1822, when the French scholar Jean-François Champollion began to decipher hieroglyphics, the Egyptian picture-writing. By then, the Egyptian language and civilization had been dead for nearly 2,000 years. The desert sands had swallowed up the smaller pyramids, and the names of the great kings and queens had been lost or forgotten. Modern archeologists sift through these ruins, searching for tiny clues that will help them to piece together the puzzles of the past. The answers to some questions are still unclear. Exactly how were the pyramids built? And what is the religious significance of the shape?
There are many theories, but we may never know for sure.

HOW MANY WORKERS DID IT TAKE?
Experts think it took 100,000 men 20 years to move all the stone for the Great Pyramid. Most of them were peasant farmers who worked on the pyramid only during the flood, which lasted three months. Another 4,000 skilled workers were on the site all year round. Their barracks have been found near the pyramid.

HOW MANY HAVEN'T BEEN DISCOVERED YET?
Some pyramids and pharaohs have been discovered only in the last few years. This gold shell comes from the so-called "Lost Pyramid" of Saqqara, which lay hidden under the desert sands until 1951. This unfinished tomb was built by Sekhemkhet, a pharaoh who was almost unknown until his name was found in the ruins. Who knows how many other pyramids still lie undiscovered beneath the shifting sands?

WERE THESE TOOLS USED TO BUILD THE GREAT PYRAMID?
When Waynman Dixon discovered the mysterious "ventilation shafts" of the Queen's Chamber in the Great Pyramid (p. 23), he also found two small tools. They are a granite pounder and a metal hook. They may have been left there by workmen. No other tools used on the Giza pyramids have survived.

Colossal statue tied to a sled with ropes   *Man clapping to keep time*   *Soldiers*

Foremen   *Men with tools*   *Men carrying water or grease*   *Man pouring liquid under the sled to grease its path*   *Four rows of men, 43 to a row, dragging the statue*

HOW DID THEY MOVE THE STONES?
There is no proof that the Egyptians used lifting machines, pulleys, or wheeled vehicles. But they definitely used sleds to move heavy objects. One of the best pieces of evidence is this drawing from the tomb of Djehutyhotep at Bersha, from 1850 B.C. It shows teams of workers dragging a huge stone statue. The Egyptians probably used similar methods to move and position the stones when building the pyramids.

Mummy case of the
lady Takhenmes,
Deir el-Bahri, 700–650 B.C.

The constellation Orion,
including the three bright
stars of Orion's belt

Scottish astronomer
Charles Piazzi Smyth

Sun or stars?

There are all sorts of strange theories about the pyramids. Many of these try to explain the link with the sun and the stars. In 1864, for example, Piazzi Smyth claimed that the pyramids were built to God's measurements. Nowadays experts agree that the pyramid was a symbolic vehicle for sending the dead king's spirit to heaven. But was the king supposed to join the sun god Re, or become "an Indestructible Star?" The pyramid texts mention both. For instance, Spell 882 says "O king, thou art this great star, the companion of Orion." It is possible that step pyramids were part of a star cult, and true pyramids were associated with the sun. The "ventilation shafts" of the Great Pyramid may have been aligned with major stars like the North Star and Orion. But some experts think their use was purely practical.

WHERE ARE THE MUMMIES?
This is a mummy case from about 650 B.C. It has always been assumed that dead kings were mummified and buried in pyramids. But if this is true, why have human remains never been found inside a pyramid burial chamber? Thieves often steal treasures, but in other tombs they usually ignore the dead bodies. Until a mummy is found in a pyramid, the possibility that some kings were not buried inside cannot be ruled out. And if these pyramids are not tombs, what other religious function did they have?

Wood covered in gold

WHERE WAS QUEEN HETEPHERES BURIED?
The only intact royal burial from the Old Kingdom found so far belonged to Queen Hetepheres. She was Sneferu's wife and Khufu's mother. Her tomb had never been robbed, and included beautiful jewelry and furniture and the queen's embalmed organs. But the sarcophagus was empty. So where was the queen's body buried? Maybe at Dahshur, or in one of Khufu's queens' pyramids.

Reconstruction of a chair from the tomb of Queen Hetepheres at Giza, c. 2600 B.C.

Lion's-paw legs

Pyramids of Nubia

Farther up the Nile River, to the south of Egypt, lies Nubia. This desert land was one of the areas where African civilization first developed. It was rich in gold and exotic goods. Nubia's position on the Nile gave it great strategic importance, and for centuries Egypt's pharaohs fought to control it. There are more than one hundred pyramids in Nubia. Over the centuries, they were all plundered for their stone, and today most of them are shapeless mounds. Like the Egyptian pyramids, they were also robbed of their treasures long ago. The first Nubian pyramids were built around 700 B.C., during a brief period when the Nubian kings ruled Egypt. They are at Kurru and Nuri, near Napata, the Nubian capital. When the capital was moved south to Meroe, around 300 B.C., pyramids were also built there. The kings and queens were mummified and buried underneath. Servants were often sacrificed and buried in the pyramid too, so that they could wait on their kings and queens in the next world.

STEEP SIDES
Nubian pyramids are smaller than the great Egyptian ones and have much steeper sides. Against the eastern face was a small funerary chapel with a gateway decorated like an Egyptian temple. Priests and pilgrims who came to honor the dead king and queen said prayers and placed offerings within the chapel. This is one of the pyramids at Meroe, in modern Sudan, as it appeared in 1820. Some 14 years later, several pyramids at Meroe were badly damaged by an Italian adventurer searching for treasure (pp. 52–53).

God Heh

Djed pillar

Ankh, a sign of life

Scepter, symbol of power and dominion

STEPPING DOWN
The burial chamber was dug under the pyramid, not built into the structure. It was approached by a long, descending flight of steps, which opened into a series of three connecting chambers cut deep into the bedrock.

GOOD LUCK CHARM
Some pyramids were built around Gebel Barkal. This strange, flat-topped peak was a sacred site for the Nubians, who called it "The Pure Mountain." This amulet was found there. It incorporates many magical symbols, including the ankh, the *djed* pillar, and a dog-headed scepter. There is also a figure of the god Heh, who represented everlasting life.

A PYRAMID FIELD AT MEROE
These are the pyramids in the northern cemetery at Meroe. They were built between 300 B.C. and about A.D. 350, when Nubia was conquered by the Axumites. By the 1st century A.D., Meroe was the center of one of Africa's great civilizations. At its peak, Nubia was a fascinating mixture of Egyptian, Greek, Roman, and central African culture. As the kingdom declined, the kings built smaller, less impressive pyramids.

Two small, intact pyramids

The tops of the big pyramids have been destroyed

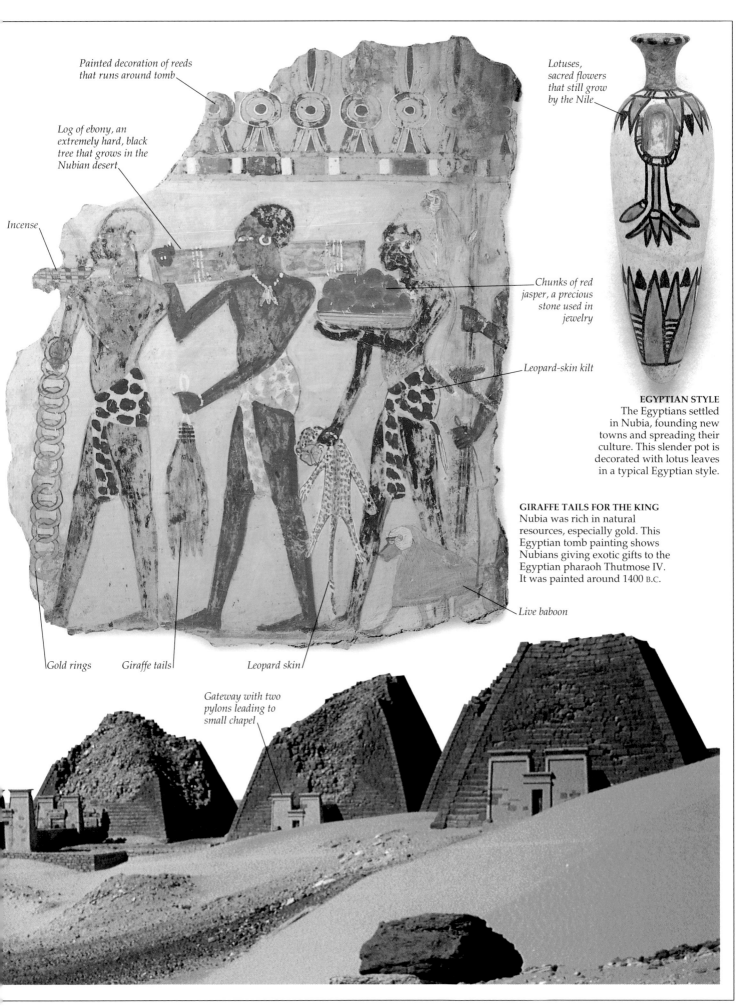

Painted decoration of reeds that runs around tomb

Lotuses, sacred flowers that still grow by the Nile

Log of ebony, an extremely hard, black tree that grows in the Nubian desert

Incense

Chunks of red jasper, a precious stone used in jewelry

Leopard-skin kilt

EGYPTIAN STYLE
The Egyptians settled in Nubia, founding new towns and spreading their culture. This slender pot is decorated with lotus leaves in a typical Egyptian style.

GIRAFFE TAILS FOR THE KING
Nubia was rich in natural resources, especially gold. This Egyptian tomb painting shows Nubians giving exotic gifts to the Egyptian pharaoh Thutmose IV. It was painted around 1400 B.C.

Live baboon

Gold rings

Giraffe tails

Leopard skin

Gateway with two pylons leading to small chapel

Pharaohs of Nubia

Gold-covered cobra, worn on king's crown to spit fire at his enemies

Around 750 B.C., when Egypt was weakened by civil wars and disorder, the Nubian kingdom prospered and grew powerful enough to conquer Egypt. For about a hundred years, the kings of Nubia were also pharaohs of Egypt. Succession to the throne was from brother to brother – not from father to son, the usual Egyptian practice. The Nubians were fascinated by the culture of Egypt, and even restored temples there. They also adopted the Egyptian tradition of being buried with shabti figures. These statues were thought to have magical powers to work for the dead person in the next world. Some were shaped like workers, others like the dead person. The Egyptians were buried with 401 shabtis – one for each day of the year, plus 36 foremen. But one Nubian king had 1,277, more than three times the usual number.

Royal cobra

Nemes headcloth, a sign of royalty

Crossed hands holding farming tools

55510

Cartouche of Anlamani

Cartouche (royal name) of Taharqo

Chapter six of the Book of the Dead

One of King Taharqo's 1,070 shabti figures, carved from translucent calcite

55512

HEAVYWEIGHT KING
King Anlamani ruled before his brother, Aspelta. This shabti figure of the king is one of 282 found in his pyramid at Nuri. They were all carved by hand, not made in a mold. The king has a massive, chunky body, with a small head and a huge *nemes* headcloth. His shabti is inscribed with chapter six of the Book of the Dead, a spell telling it to do agricultural work in the next world.

NO BED
The best-preserved pyramid at Nuri belongs to King Aspelta. This is one of the 300 shabti figures found inside. Aspelta was one of the first Nubian rulers to be buried in a coffin and a stone sarcophagus. Earlier kings were laid to rest in beds.

The great Taharqo

King Taharqo is the most famous Nubian king. He ruled over Nubia and Egypt from 690 to 664 B.C., at the height of the 25th dynasty. He is even mentioned in the Bible. Taharqo built many monuments and temples in both lands. His huge pyramid at Nuri was probably inspired by the great Giza pyramids, which he could see from his palace at Memphis.

MAGIC TABLETS
These are foundation deposits with the names of kings written on them. After a ritual ceremony, they were placed in the foundations at the four corners of the king's pyramid, to help it last forever.

55563

Taharqo wears a khat, a baglike wig cover

False beard worn only on formal occasions

Farming tools held against chest

FEATHER CROWN
Taharqo was a powerful military leader. This painting by Winifred Brunton (p. 42) shows him as he may have looked in life. He is wearing a leopard-skin cape and an elaborate feather crown.

RUINS AT NURI
An English explorer drew this picture of the pyramids at Nuri in the 1820s. There are 20 large pyramids for kings there, plus another 53 smaller pyramids for queens. They were built between about 700 and 300 B.C. All are made from local red sandstone, a soft rock that has not weathered very well. Even 170 years ago the pyramids were badly ruined.

This is Taharqo's biggest shabti, 2 ft (60 cm) tall

Shabti figure of the pharaoh Senkamanisken, made of faience, a sort of glazed earthenware

55506

Shabti figure of King Taharqo carved from speckled granite

Royal cobra

Nemes headcloth

King holds flail and crook

Stone shabti figure of King Senkamanisken

COPIES OF THE KING
King Senkamanisken was buried with smaller shabti figures than his grandfather, Taharqo. But he had a few more – 1,277 in all. Senkamanisken ruled from 643 to 623 B.C. By the time he took the throne, Nubia had lost control of Egypt.

Foundation deposit from the pyramid of King Senkamanisken at Nuri

A queen's treasure

OF ALL THE HUNDREDS OF PYRAMIDS in Egypt and Nubia, a hoard of treasure has been found in only one. The pyramid, at Meroe in the Sudan, belonged to Queen Amanishakheto, who ruled Nubia in the first century B.C. In 1834, the Italian adventurer Giuseppe Ferlini found a magnificent collection of jewelry in a secret chamber near the top of the tomb. At that time, the pyramid was one of the best preserved in Nubia. But Ferlini was not an archeologist. He tore the pyramid to pieces in his greedy hunt for more treasure.

Crown of tall feathers

Cobra

Sun disk

Ram-headed god Amun

Gold sheet decorated with gold wire

ARMS FULL OF BRACELETS
Ferlini found five pairs of bracelets. Nubian queens were shown wearing many bracelets, and Amanishakheto may have worn all ten at the same time. This is Queen Nawidamak, Amanishakheto's predecessor.

JINGLE BELLS
The queen wore this shield ring to show her devotion to the god Amun. The drop-shaped pendants made a jingly noise, which was probably intended to please Amun and repel evil spirits.

Bracelet with a small image of Amun before a chapel

Engraving published by Richard Lepsius in the 1840s

Gold inlaid with colored glass

String of wadjet *eyes*

ALL EYES TOGETHER
The *wadjet* eye was a very popular good luck charm. It was also known as the Eye of Horus. Egyptians and Nubians wore an eye amulet to protect them from evil. These *wadjet* eyes have been linked in a chain, together with a hanging pendant shaped like a lotus flower.

SPREADING HER WINGS
The goddess Mut is the centerpiece of this beautiful gold bracelet. She is holding out her feathered wings in a protective gesture. Nubian queens identified themselves with Mut, believing she was the wife of their most important god, Amun.

Upside-down lotus flower

Goddess Mut

Cobra decoration

Smaller images of the goddess Mut spreading her wings

Sun disk

Loops show that pieces were part of a complex chain or collar necklace

SIGNS OF LIFE
Cut from a sheet of solid gold, these eight ankh symbols form the links of a chain worn around the neck. The ankh was the sacred sign of life and was usually reserved for kings, queens, and gods. Only they had the power to give or take away life. The origin of the looped cross is uncertain, but it may represent the tie straps of a sandal.

Row of royal cobras ready to strike

Lion head

Sun disk

The front of a chapel or shrine

RAM POWER
This shield ring is dominated by a ram's head. It represents Amun, the supreme state god of Nubia. He is standing in front of a small shrine or chapel. The gold granules around the ram's neck form a long necklace from which a miniature image of Amun hangs. The name Amun means "hidden one," and the Nubians believed he lived inside the sacred mountain Gebel Barkal (p. 48). In hieroglyphs, the sign for the ram's head means power and prestige.

EVERYDAY JEWELRY
There were nine shield rings in Amanishakheto's jewelry collection. This one features the lion-headed god Apedemak. It was not worn on the fingers like an ordinary ring. Instead he queen must have attached it to her hair and hung it over her forehead. Scientific examination has revealed traces of wear on the queen's jewelry. This proves that it wasn't made specially for her tomb. She must have worn it in her daily life.

Ram-headed god Amun

Miniature image of god Amun hanging from necklace

Pyramids of Mexico

BEFORE THE ARRIVAL OF EUROPEANS, Mexico and Central America were home to a wide variety of different peoples and empires. Over the centuries they built thousands of pyramids, usually with steps or terraces rising to a flat top. Most of the pyramids were temples, often arranged in complexes with many smaller religious buildings. Priests climbed the stairs to high altars where they conducted sacred rites, including human sacrifice. A few pyramids were constructed over tombs. Some of the most magnificent structures were built by the Mayan people in southern Mexico between the 3rd and the 9th century A.D. The great Aztec pyramids were destroyed by the Spanish *conquistadores* (conquerors) who invaded Mexico in 1519.

OLMEC FROWN
The Olmecs created the first great civilization of ancient Mexico. They were highly skilled at stoneworking and built massive earthen pyramid mounds at La Venta as early as 1000 B.C. They also carved beautiful masks as offerings to their gods. These masks have huge features and are usually frowning. The Olmecs' religious beliefs influenced later cultures like the Maya and the Zapotec.

THE BIG ONES
Here are some major pyramid sites in Central America. It is not a huge area, but it includes high, cool valleys and steamy lowland jungles. Many sites have never been excavated. For instance, hundreds of small pyramids are still hidden in the dense jungle of Belize and the Yucatán Peninsula.

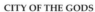

Map labels: Gulf of Mexico; Uxmal; Chichén Itzá; Yucatán Peninsula; Teotihuacan; Tenochtitlán; Sayil; El Tajín; Mexico; Xpuhil; Palenque; Belize; Monte Albán; Tikal; Pacific Ocean; Guatemala; Honduras; Copán; El Salvador; ▲ Pyramid site

MEANWHILE, IN SOUTH AMERICA...
On the north coast of Peru, the Moche people built two great pyramids, the Huaca del Sol and the Huaca del Luna. They used sun-baked mud bricks laid in layers. The pyramids had two or three levels, and were coated in plaster and painted with colorful murals. The Moche also made fine pottery. This vessel is shaped like a warrior.

COMPARING SIZES
The bases of the Pyramid of the Sun at Teotihuacan and the Great Pyramid of Egypt are almost the same size. But the Mexican pyramid is only about half as high. It is made of about 2.5 million tons of stone and earth, compared with 6.5 million tons of stone in the Great Pyramid.

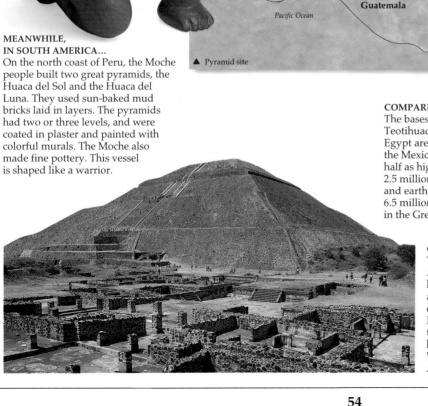

CITY OF THE GODS
Teotihuacan is the most impressive ancient city in the Americas. This huge metropolis once may have been home to 250,000 people. Its many buildings and pyramids are carefully laid out on a strict grid plan. The wide Avenue of the Dead runs between the two biggest structures, the Pyramid of the Sun and the Pyramid of the Moon. This is the Pyramid of the Sun, built around A.D. 150. It appears to have no internal chambers, though there is a cave inside it. Who built this great city? When the Spanish asked the Aztecs, they said, "The gods."

RAIN TOWN
Between A.D. 300 and A.D. 900, the city of El Tajín was the most important center on the Veracruz coast of Mexico. This lush area was famous for its maize, cocoa, and cotton. The town itself was named after the rain god, Tajín. This imaginative painting by the Mexican artist Diego Rivera (1886–1957) shows two pyramids. The one on the right is the Pyramid of the Niches.

A detail from the fresco *Offering of Fruits, Tobacco, Cacao and, Vanilla to the Emperor,* by Diego Rivera, 1950.

A NICHE A DAY
The Pyramid of the Niches at El Tajín rises in six tiers. Each tier contains rows of niches. There are 365 in all, one for each day of the year. Offerings or figures of gods may have been placed in the niches.

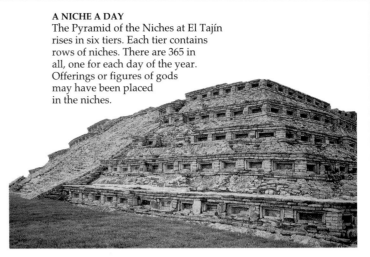

ZAPOTEC GOD
The Zapotec people made their capital at Monte Albán in the Oaxaca region of Mexico. Between 600 B.C. and A.D. 800, they built a remarkable city of pyramid temples and tombs there. The tombs have niches where clay funeral urns were placed. On this urn the rain god Cocijo wears a typical Zapotec feathered headdress.

Elaborate feathered headdress

Urn was built up from layers of clay slabs

The rain god Cocijo, wearing ear-studs and sticking out his forked tongue

Urn is made around a cylinder that held food offerings or ashes

Mayan pyramids

BETWEEN THE 3RD AND THE 9TH CENTURY A.D., the Mayas built pyramids all across eastern Mexico and into modern Belize, Guatemala, Honduras, and El Salvador. Made of stone blocks held together with strong lime mortar, these pyramids were built at steeper angles than Egyptian ones. The stair-cases sometimes got narrower as they rose, to make the pyramids seem even taller and steeper. This also drew attention to the rituals performed in the temple chamber at the top. Crowds gathered at the base, but only priests could climb to the sacred heights. The Mayas were skilled astronomers and laid out their pyramids according to the sun, moon, and stars. They also developed yearly and sacred calendars, a system of mathematics, and their own language of picture-writing, or "glyphs." It has still not been fully deciphered.

CITY KINGDOM
The Maya did not have a single capital or king. Instead each city governed itself under its own ruler. One important later city was Chichén Itzá in the Yucatán Peninsula. There were many major religious and administrative buildings there, including the famous pyramid El Castillo. The architecture of the stone pillars shows the influence of the Toltecs, a neighbouring culture. People were thrown to their deaths in the sacred Well of Sacrifice.

DANCING GODS
These drawings show two gods shared by most Central American people. On his nightly journey beneath the earth, the sun god became the jaguar god of the underworld. The black spots on his fur symbolized the stars. The serpent Quetzalcoatl was thought to express sacred power. A person's head is often shown emerging from his open mouth, to link this sacred creature to the human world.

Jaguar god

Quetzalcoatl

JAGUAR POT
Very few Mayan wall paintings remain. But we can get some idea of their quality from the decorated ceramics that have survived. Pots for the rich or for religious use were covered with stucco and then painted while still wet. This one shows a jaguar, admired for its skill in hunting and its strength, ferocity, and cunning.

Temple chamber where priests conducted sacred rituals

Entrance to temple chamber

The stone was coated with plaster and then painted, possibly blood-red

The four staircases probably symbolized the division of the cosmos into four quadrants

CRACKING THE CODE

For over a hundred years, researchers struggled to understand the mysterious Mayan glyphs. Only in the last twenty years have they started to break the code. There are many stone inscriptions. But most of the Mayan books, called codices, were burned in 1562 by a Spanish priest who claimed they were the works of the devil. Only four survived. These were written and painted on bark paper folded in sections. They have helped us to understand the Mayan calendars and mathematics. These five gods are from the Codex Tro-Cortesianus. The bars and dots are glyphs for numbers.

FEATHERED SERPENT

The first known god of Mexico was Quetzalcoatl, the feathered serpent. This is one of the seven serpent figures on the northern stairs of El Castillo pyramid at Chichén Itzá. At the autumn equinox, about September 23 every year, the sun shines through the mouths of all seven serpents.

LOST CITIES

In the 800s, the Mayan civilization went through a spectacular collapse. No one really knows why. Ravaged by war and famine, the cities were abandoned one by one. The jungle plants took over the temples, and the statues were swallowed by the undergrowth. These lost cities were rediscovered only recently. This is a photo of El Castillo pyramid at Chichén Itzá, taken by an English explorer around 1900.

Pyramid is 79 ft (24 m) high

STEPPING THE DAYS AWAY

This model shows El Castillo pyramid at Chichén Itzá. It has four staircases, three with 91 steps and one with 92. That makes a total of 365 steps, one for each day of the year.

Single northern staircase on inner Toltec pyramid

Outer Mayan pyramid has four staircases

INNER TEMPLES

Mexican pyramids were often enlarged by new rulers. In this way, they grew bigger and bigger. In 1930, Mexican archeologists discovered an earlier temple inside Chichén Itzá pyramid. Probably built by the Toltecs, it also has nine levels, but only one staircase. Inside the temple chamber are a magnificent jaguar throne and a sculpture on which offerings were placed.

Nine terraces

Continued on next page

Blood-letting and sacrifice

Bloody rituals were a vital part of Mayan life. The Mayas believed that to keep the cosmic order, the gods needed to be fed with blood. In return, the gods would provide good harvests and prevent natural disasters like earthquakes. One mural shows prisoners of war being tortured by having their fingernails pulled out. Human sacrifice may have been introduced to the Mayas by the warlike Toltecs. The victims were prisoners of war, slaves, or children bought especially for the occasion. The priest who performed the sacrifice was helped by four old men who held the victim's arms and legs while the chest was ripped open. The priests performed these sacrifices during special festivals in the sacred calendar.

SPILLING YOUR OWN BLOOD
Mayan nobles mutilated themselves in special blood-letting ceremonies. They passed needles or stingray spines through parts of the body and collected the blood to smear on statues. Men usually pierced their penises. This sculpture from Yaxchilán, (south of Tikal) shows Lady Xoc passing a string of thorns through her tongue. The ruler Shield Jaguar looks on.

Glyphs from a wooden beam on the Temple of the Giant Jaguar in Tikal, Guatemala

PUBLIC ADDRESS
There are five major pyramid complexes at Tikal, Guatemala. This is the Temple of the Giant Jaguar, the tallest of all the Mayan pyramids. It rises steeply to a height of 230 ft (70 m). The chamber at the top was designed to amplify the priests' voices, so they could be heard by spectators at the base. The tomb of a Mayan lord, Ah Cacan, was beneath the pyramid.

OVAL PYRAMID
The Pyramid of the Magician at Uxmal, Mexico, has curved corners. It was built in five distinct phases between the 6th and the 10th century. The ceremonial stairway on the west side leads to the broad temple chamber. The entrance is ornately decorated and looks like the mouth of a great monster.

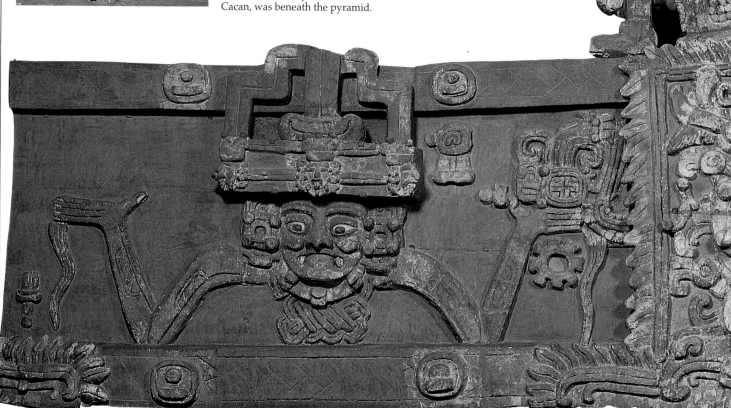

DOORWAY TO DATES

Mayan temple doors were spanned by wooden beams. The wood can be dated by the radiocarbon process. This process helps scholars to confirm the dates of Mayan history, which are still not very clear. These details from a wooden beam are glyphs.

A glyph from a wooden beam on the Temple of the Giant Jaguar, Tikal, Guatemala

King, wearing a feathered crown

Members of the royal family

Nobles, priests, and warriors

Merchants, artists, and craftsworkers

Peasant-farmers, laborers, and slaves

MAYAN SOCIAL PYRAMID

A modern Mexican artist painted this pyramid to show the different classes of Mayan society. It is done in the style of the beautiful frescoes found at Bonampak, Guatemala. Each important Mayan city had its own ruler or king, who was regarded by his people as a living god. To live up to his reputation, the king built splendid palaces and temples.

JUNGLE RUINS

Between 1839 and 1842, John Stephens and Frederick Catherwood made two famous expeditions to explore Mayan ruins. Jungle travel was dangerous, and they both suffered bad bouts of malaria. Their writings and drawings revealed the full splendor of the lost civilization. This lithograph shows a pyramid in Tulum, Mexico.

MYSTERIOUS GODS

This is a reconstruction of a frieze from Campeche, Mexico. Traces of color suggest that the original was brightly painted. Very little is known about the bewildering variety of Mayan gods.

Aztec pyramids

THE AZTECS RULED the last great empire of Central America. They called themselves *Mexica* and made their capital at Tenochtitlán, now Mexico City. When the Spanish *conquistadores* entered Tenochtitlán in 1519, they found one of the largest cities in the world. They were impressed by its beauty, cleanliness, and order. But as they approached the huge ceremonial center, the Spaniards were horrified by the smell of blood. The Aztecs used their pyramids for human sacrifice, which they believed provided vital energy needed for the workings of the universe. In the last years of their empire, thousands of victims, mostly prisoners of war, were sacrificed each year. The Aztecs built their pyramids from a core of adobe mud bricks faced with stone held together by mortar. None of them were very high. The tallest, the Great Temple of Tenochtitlán, was only a fifth of the height of the Great Pyramid at Giza.

Tezcatlipoca

Huitzilopochtli

REPAYING THE GODS
The top of the pyramid was a place of bloody sacrifice. Here the priests removed the still-beating heart of the victim. Then they threw the body down the steps, and the limbs were hacked off and ceremonially eaten. The Aztecs believed that the world had been created by their gods' own sacrifice. These terrible rituals were their gifts of thanks.

The snake was associated with the god Quetzalcoatl, whose name meant "feathered serpent"

SACRIFICIAL KNIFE
The victim's heart was cut out with a stone knife. The Aztecs had no iron and made their tools from razor-sharp flint or obsidian, a volcanic glass. This flint blade is decorated with a turquoise mosaic of a snake, a symbol of sacred power. The Aztecs excelled at mosaic work using jade, coral, shell, and turquoise.

Tlaloc

Paynal

WARRIOR GODS
The Aztecs waged war constantly to provide captives for sacrifice. Their many gods were often depicted as warriors. Most gods were associated with the forces of nature. These four are in an Aztec book, the Codex Florentino. Huitzilopochtli was a god of war and the sun, and the protector the *Mexica* (Aztecs). Tezcatlipoca was an invisible god associated with the night and the north. Paynal was a god of speed, and Tlaloc was a rain god worshiped by farmers.

Massive ear-stud

Shrine to Huitzilopochtli, god of war and the sun

Shrine to Tlaloc, god of rain

STONE FACE
Masks were an important part of Aztec life and were often worn during festivals. Stone masks were too heavy to wear but may have been placed over the faces of mummies to protect them in the afterlife. Finely carved stone masks were also placed in temples as offerings to the gods. This one is probably Xipe Totec, god of springtime and vegetation.

Sacrifices were made inside shrine

TENAYUCA PYRAMID
The pyramid temple of Tenayuca had two staircases leading to two shrines. Sacrifices made in the blue shrine were meant to guarantee a good harvest. Sacrifices in the red shrine were made to ensure victory in war, which provided a regular supply of prisoners for sacrifice. Huge crowds gathered at the base of the pyramid to watch the sacrificial rituals.

Pyramid was enlarged several times between A.D. 1300 and 1500

The pyramid lives on

Four and a half thousand years after the Great Pyramid rose on Egypt's desert horizon, a different kind of pyramid is appearing on city skylines. Modern pyramids are not made of millions of tons of stone. It does not take thousands of workers to build them, and they represent big business, not the spiritual realm of the dead. New materials like reinforced concrete and smoked glass supported by steel girders mean that huge structures can be built with a minimum of effort. There is something special about the pyramid shape that has inspired architects, artists, and designers throughout history. As a geometric shape, it is the supreme symbol of natural balance and harmony. Built on a grand scale, it gives the impression of something superhuman, built by the gods. The eternal magic of the pyramid is destined to live on and on.

THE ROME PYRAMID
The most impressive ancient pyramid in Europe is in Rome. It was built by Caius Cestius, an important official who died in 12 B.C. He is buried beneath the pyramid.

The all-seeing eye

Detail from dollar bill

13 rows of bricks symbolizing the 13 original states of the U.S.A.

Roman numerals for 1776, the year of the Declaration of Independence

A NEW ERA
Since 1935, the one-dollar bill has included a picture of a pyramid from the Great Seal of the United States. It represents permanence and strength. The all-seeing eye of God looks out from the pyramid's summit. The Latin motto refers to the beginning of a new era after the Declaration of Independence in 1776. The 13 rows of bricks at the pyramid's base stand for the 13 original states.

PYRAMID POWER
This greenhouse is in the botanical gardens in Sydney, Australia. The pyramid shape ensures that a large surface area of glass faces the sun. Many people believe that the pyramid shape itself can generate hidden power or energy. They claim that a blunt razor blade left at the center of a pyramid will be miraculously sharpened!

One-dollar bill

SETTING THE SCENE
The simple elegance of ancient Egyptian art has inspired many modern artists. The British artist David Hockney designed stage sets for Mozart's opera "The Magic Flute" in 1978. He used the pyramid shape to create a modern sense of grandeur.

A TOMB FOR THE NIGHT

The latest "Great Pyramid" was built not by a pharaoh of Egypt but by an American businessman, Steve Wynn. It is the Luxor Hotel in Las Vegas, which opened in 1993. It has 5,000 rooms, is 30 stories tall, and cost $300 million to build. The outside is made of black mirrored glass. Before it crouches a replica of the Sphinx, even larger than the original, surrounded by plastic palm trees. The fantasy world continues inside the hotel, where a fake Nile River runs through an Egyptian theme park complete with virtual reality sets and a video game arcade.

SHAKE-PROOF

Built in 1970, the Transamerica Pyramid in San Francisco rises to a height of 843 ft (257 m). The pyramid shape is part of a special design to combat the deadly shaking of earthquakes, which can topple high buildings in a few seconds.

REACH FOR THE SKY

The Canary Wharf Tower is the tallest building in Britain. It is topped by a pyramid that dominates the London skyline. The pyramid contains the air-conditioning systems and elevator machinery for the 50-story skyscraper below it. A flashing light at the tip warns aircraft to keep clear.

The pyramid reflects the old buildings and the sky

ENTERING THE PYRAMID

At the time of the French king Louis XIV, there were unfulfilled plans to build a pyramid on the grounds of the Louvre palace in Paris. This dream was realized three centuries later in 1989, when the Louvre Pyramid was opened by President François Mitterand. The architect, I. M. Pei, designed it as a new entrance to the Louvre, which is now a museum. It forms a visitor's reception hall that leads to the main galleries. The modern design was very controversial, because the pyramid is surrounded by such historic buildings. But it has proved to be very popular.

Glass is held in place by oxidized steel girders

Sides rise at the same angle as the Great Pyramid

Index

A

Abu Roash, 9
Abusir, 24, 38
Abydos, 29
Amanishakheto, Queen, 52-53
Amenemhat I, 40
Amenemhat III, 40, 42, 43
Amenhotep, 33
Amun, 26, 41, 52, 53
Anherkhau, 34
Anlamani, 50
Anubis, 45
Apedemak, 53
Aspelta, 50
Aswan, 32, 43
Atet, 15
Axumites, 48
Aztecs, 6, 54, 60-61

B

basalt, 32
Belize, 54, 56
Belzoni, Giovanni, 22
Bent Pyramid, 14, 15
Bersha, 46
Black Pyramid, 42
boats, funeral, 28-29
Bonampak, 59
boning rods, 30
Book of the Dead, 22, 29, 44, 50
bricks, 33, 40
Brunton, Winifred, 39, 42, 43, 51
Bugentef, 44
building pyramids, 32-37

C

Cairo, 20, 21
Campeche, 59
Canary Wharf Tower, 63
capstones, 43, 44-45
cartouches, 18, 34
casing stones, 32, 36
Catherwood, Frederick, 59
Caviglia, Giovanni, 27
Central America, 6, 54-61
Cestius, Caius, 62
Champollion, J.-F., 46
Chichén Itzá, 6, 56, 57
Cocijo, 55
Codex Florentino, 61
conquistadores, 54, 60
cubits, 30

D

Dahshur, 14, 40, 42, 47
Deir el-Bahri, 35, 41
Dixon, Waynman, 46
Djehutyhotep, 46
Djoser, 7, 10-13, 42
dolerite, 34
dollar bills, 62
dummy buildings, 12, 13

E

Edfu temple, 31
El Castillo, 56, 57
El Lahun, 40, 42
El Lisht, 8, 40
El Salvador, 56
El Tajín, 55
Eye of Horus, 28, 52

F

Ferlini, Giuseppe, 52
Flinders Petrie, W.M., 14, 18
foundations, 30, 31, 50
funerals, 24

G

Gebel Barkal, 48, 53
Giza, 6, 16-21, 26-27, 50
glyphs, 56-57, 58-59
granite, 32, 34
Great Pyramid, 14, 16-17, 20-21, 54
construction, 20, 32, 36
entrance, 22
explorers, 23
Grand Gallery, 22, 23
King's Chamber, 20, 23, 32
layout, 23
mortuary temples, 24
names, 18
planning, 30
Queen's Chamber, 23
"ventilation shafts," 23, 46, 47
Guatemala, 56, 58, 59

H

Hatshepsut, Queen, 41
Hawara, 43
Heh, 48
Heliopolis, 44, 45
Herodotus, 36
Hesire, 31
Hetepheres, 9, 47
Hetepirkara, 38
hieroglyphs, 18, 38, 46
Hockney, David, 62
Honduras, 56
Horemakhet, 27
Horus, 18, 27, 28, 38, 52
human sacrifices, 6, 54, 58, 60
Hunefer, 29, 44

I J

Imhotep, 10, 11, 13
Ipi, 32, 35
Java, 6
jewelry, 40, 42, 43, 52-53

K

Kagemni, 28
Karnak, 26, 41
Katep, 9
Khaemwaset, 32
Khafra, 6, 16-19, 26-27
Khamerernebty, 19
Khufu, 14, 16-19, 20, 21, 23, 28, 29
Kurru, 48

L

La Venta, 54
laborers, 8, 36, 46
Las Vegas, 63
Lauer, Jean-Philippe, 12
limestone, 32
"Lost Pyramid," 46
Louvre Pyramid, 63
Luxor, 26

M

Maat, 45
Maiden Castle, 6
Mallorca, 17
manacles, 32
Marksburg, 20
mason, 7, 10, 56-57
meals, 38-39, 42-43
medallion, 31
merlons, 26
Mespelbrunn, 18
metalwork, 60-61
miter, 23
moats, 26, 28, 36
mon, 37
motte and bailey, 8-9
mold, 61
Mowbray family, 31
murder holes, 28
music, 44-45
Muslims, 16-17, 34-35
Mycenae, 6

N O

Napata, 48
Napoleon I, Emperor, 23
Nawidamak, Queen, 52
Nefer-Maat, 15
Neferirkara, 38
Nefertiabet, 25
Neith, 39
New Kingdom, 6, 44
Nile River, 7, 8, 16, 28, 30, 32, 43
Nofret, 14
Nubia, 26, 41, 42, 45, 48-53
Nuri, 48, 50, 51
Nyuserra, 38
oars, 28
offerings, 24-25
officials, 8
Old Kingdom, 6, 8, 39, 40
Olmecs, 54
Orion, 47
Osiris, 29, 32
ostraca, 32

P

paintings, 15, 24-25, 33, 34, 41, 56
papyrus, 31, 32, 39
Pei, I. M., 63
Pepy I, 39
Pepy II, 39
Peru, 54
pharaohs, 8-9, 18-19, 50-1
planning pyramids, 30-31
Ptah, 11, 32
Pyramid of the Giant Jaguar, 58, 59
Pyramid of the Magician 58
Pyramid of the Niches, 55
Pyramid of the Sun, 54
Pyramid Texts, 7, 22, 47
pyramidions, 44-45

Q R

quarries, 32
queens' pyramids, 17, 19, 21, 51
Quetzalcoatl, 56, 57, 60
Radjedef, 9, 29
Rahotep, 14
ramps, 36-37
Ramses II, 32
Raneferef, 38
Re, 7, 28, 39, 44, 45, 47
reed boats, 28
Rekhmire, 30, 33, 34, 36
Rhind Papyrus, 30
Rivera, Diego, 55
robbers, 22, 38, 40, 43
Rome, 62
Rosetta Stone, 32

S

sacrifices, 6, 54, 58, 60
Sahura, 38, 39
sandstone, 32, 51
Saqqara, 10-13, 28, 32, 39, 46
sarcophagus, 22
Sat-Hathor III, 40
scaffolding, 34
scribes, 31
sed festival, 12, 41
Sekhemkhet, 46
Senkamanisken, 51
Sennedjsui, 25
Senusret I, 40
Senusret II, 40
Senusret III, 28, 42
servants, 8, 9
Seshemnufer, 24
Seven Wonders of the Ancient World, 21
shabti figures, 50, 51
Sinai Peninsula, 14, 21
sleds, 37, 46

Smyth, Charles Piazzi, 47
Sneferu, 14-15, 47
South America, 54
Spain, 54, 60
Sphinx, 6, 16, 18, 26-27, 63
stars, 47
statues, 9, 11
stelae, 25, 44
Step Pyramid, 10-13, 42
step pyramids, 7, 14, 47
Stephens, John, 59
stone, 32, 34
Sudan, 6, 44, 48
Sun, 6, 7, 38, 47, 57
Sydney, 62

T

Taharquo, 50-51
Takhenmes, 47
Temple of Siva, 6
temples, 24-5, 38, 39, 54, 56
Tenayuca, 61
Tenochtitlán, 60
Teotihuacan, 54
Thebes, 41
Thoth, 21
Thutmose III, 35
Thutmose IV, 26, 27, 49
Ti, 24
Tikal, 58, 59
Toltecs, 56, 57, 58
tools, 30, 34-35, 46, 60
Transamerica Pyramid 63
treasures, 22
Tulum, 59
Tura, 32, 38
Tutankhamun, 6, 22
Twain, Mark, 20

U-Z

Udjahor, 45
Unas, 22, 32
United States, 62, 63
Userkaf, 38, 39
Uxmal, 58
Valley of the Kings, 22
"ventilation shafts," 23, 46, 47
Vyse, Howard, 38
writing, 22, 46, 56-57, 58-59
Wynn, Steve, 63
Yucatán, 54, 56
Zapotecs, 54, 55

Acknowledgments

Dorling Kindersley would like to thank:
The staff of the Department of Egyptian Antiquities at the British Museum, London, in particular John Taylor, Stephen Quirke, Carol Andrews, Jeffrey Spencer, Virginia Hewitt, Tony Brandon, Bob Dominey, and John Hayman; the British Museum Photographic Department, especially Ivor Kerslake; Angela Thomas and Arthur Boulton at the Bolton Museum; Robert Bauval; Jean-Phillipe Lauer; Helena Spiteri, and Linda Martin for editorial help; Sharon Spencer, Susan St. Louis, Isaac Zamora, and Ivan Finnegan for design help.
Additional photography by Peter Anderson (25ar, 36–37, 41br, 47l), Stan Bean (12–13), Janet Peckham (46cr), Dave Rudkin (55b), Karl Shone.
Maps by Simone End (6cr, 8r, 54c)
Illustrations by John Woodcock (18bl, 21t, 41c, 54br), Sergio Momo (54c)
Index by Hilary Bird

Picture credits
a=above, b=below, c=center, l=left, r=right

Ayeshah Abdel-Haleem: 22br; Ancient Art and Architecture Collection: 37ar, 41ar; Stan Bean / Egyptian Museum, San José, Ca: 12-13b; Biblioteca Medicea Laurenziania / Photo - Scardigli: 60ar, 61al; Phot. Bibl. Nat., Paris / Codex Telleriano-Remensis: 61cl; Bibliothèque du Musée de l'Homme: 57ac; J.Allan Cash Photolibrary: 62cr; J.L.Charmet: 59cl; G. Dagli Orti: 59ar; Vivien Davis: 48cl, 48-49b; e.t.archive: 7c, 22cl, (detail) 43bl, 55ar; Mary Evans Picture Library: 16al, 17cr, 22al, 42al, 47c, 60c; Francis Firth/Royal Photographic Society, Bath (The Southern stone pyramid of Dahshoor from the South West): 14cr; Gallimard Jeunesse: 17ar, 18c; Robert Harding Picture Library: 47br, 63al, 63ar; © David Hockney/Photo-Guy Gravett: 62bl; Hutchison Library: 6bl, 58cl, /Pate: 6ar, 57ar; Image Bank/Luis Castañeda: 58ac, /Derek Berwin: 63cl; INAH: 57al; H.Lewandowski/ Photo - R.M.N: 9al; Jürgen Liepe: 11br, 18al, 18cr, 38br, 39cl, 46cl; Mansell Collection: (detail) 21bcr, 37cr, 38cl; © Metropolitan Museum of Art, Gift of Edward S. Harkness, 1914 (14.3.17): 40l; Daniel Moignot, P.L.J. Gallimard-Larousse: 37al; Museum Expedition. Courtesy of Museum of Fine Arts, Boston: 19r; National Palace, Mexico City/Photo - e.t. archive (detail, Diego Rivera 'Totonac Civilisation') - Reproduccion authorizada por el Instituto Nacional de Bellas Artes y Literatura: 55al; James Putnam: 7cr, 17al, 19al, 20ar, 21c, 42cl, 43cl, 51ac; R.M.N: 25br; John Ross: 12al; Royal Museum of Scotland: 56bl; Royal Observatory, Edinburgh: 47 ar; John Sandford/Science Photo Library: 47acr; Staatlichen Museen zu Berlin Preussischer Kulturbesitz Agyptisches Museum/Photo - Margarete Busing/Bildarchiv: 52ar, 52b, 52c, 53a, 53b, 53br; Tony Stone Images: 63b; Werner Forman Archive: 14ar, 15al, 22bl, 31cl, 32cr, (detail) 35cl, (detail) 35ac, 39ar; Michel Zabé: 56-57b, 57cr, 58-59b, 60-61b; Zefa: 54bl, /J.Schörken: 56al.

Every effort has been made to trace the copyright holders and we apologise in advance for any unintentional omissions. We would be pleased to insert the appropriate acknowledgment in any subsequent edition of this publication.